*Is Liberalism Dead?
and Other Essays*

Is Liberalism Dead?

AND OTHER ESSAYS

BY

MAX SAVELLE

UNIVERSITY OF WASHINGTON PRESS

Seattle and London

ACKNOWLEDGMENTS

PART I. "Is Liberalism Dead?" was first published in *The Historian*, XX (November, 1957), 3-23. "Prolegomena to a History of Liberalism in Eighteenth-Century Anglo-America" appeared in the *Bucknell Review*, IX (December, 1960), 224-46. "Benjamin Franklin and American Liberalism" was originally published in *Western Humanities Review*, XVIII (Summer, 1964), 197-209.

PART II. "The Appearance of an American Attitude toward External Affairs, 1750-1775" is from the *American Historical Review*, LII (July, 1947), 655-66. "The Imperial School of American Colonial Historians" originally appeared in the *Indiana Magazine of History*, XLV (June, 1949), 123-34. "Nationalism and Other Loyalties in the American Revolution" was first published in the *American Historical Review*, LXVII (July, 1962), 901-23.

PART III. "The Flight from Reason" is a review article of *Man the Measure* by E. Kahler and *Condition of Man* by L. Mumford. It appeared in the *Journal of Modern History*, XVII (June, 1945), 153-62. "The Philosophy of the General: Toynbee Versus the Naturalists" is a review article of Volumes I-X of

[v]

Acknowledgments

Study of History by A. J. Toynbee. It was first published in the *Pacific Historical Review*, XXV (February, 1956), 55-67. "Historian's Progress or The Quest for Sancta Sophia" was Max Savelle's presidential address delivered at the 1957 meeting of the Pacific Coast Branch of the American Historical Association. It was published in the *Pacific Historical Review*, XXVII (February, 1958), 1-26.

CONTENTS

[vii]

INTRODUCTION

THE following reviews and articles by Professor Max Savelle are brought together here in the name of his two generations of graduate students to express our deep respect and warm affection for him. Professor Savelle taught at Columbia University from 1926 to 1932, at Stanford University from 1932 to 1946, and at the University of Washington from 1946 to 1967. During those years he has guided through the perils of graduate study an impressive number of students who will always value the distinctive liberal mark of that training. Max Savelle permitted each of his students to explore the sources of early American history freely—according to his own interests, needs, and talents—and to arrive at independent interpretive positions, as long as he adhered to the canons of sound scholarship. For some students, such freedom led away from colonial history altogether, but for most it opened the exciting world of a society's beginnings.

It is to the liberal spirit of Max Savelle that his students dedicate this collection of his writings on the history and problem of liberalism in America.

Professor Savelle's liberalism is deeply rooted in his study of America's beginnings, and finds its intellectual origins in the century of his concentrated study—the eighteenth. In that Age of Enlightenment, Professor Savelle found a dedication to a common-sense reason that disciplined the mind of man without hampering its imagination. For him, the power of eighteenth-century reason freed man from the limitations of formal logic of the past centuries while it checked the dangerous conclusions of later romantic moods. The Enlightenment offered, too, a period when the dignity of man soared as his capabilities for self-improvement unfolded. For the first time in centuries of human experience, the well-being of the individual profoundly concerned society, and man's right to his own independent views was protected and valued.

Like Thomas Jefferson, Professor Savelle assigns man personal, direct responsibility for his conduct, but, like Jefferson, he also found the environmentalism of the Enlightenment appealing. This new land did indeed offer men an exciting opportunity for experimentation with social and political institutions, out of which came the views of the revolutionary generation, which Professor Savelle warmly supports.

But the intellect revealed in this book is of the twentieth century. In the idiom of his own day, Professor Savelle has staunchly defended the proposition that man is free and responsible. He has found the determinism suggested by the social scientists and the negation of reason offered by some psychologists to be both frightening and indefensible. In the first instance the quantification of man's behavior has led to suggestions of the ease with which man might be controlled, and in the second case the study of the emotional side of man's behavior has subordinated reason to what Professor Savelle has styled "a new romanticism." This spirit of liberalism with its delicate defense of personal freedom is developed, defined, and defended in these essays.

This material has been selected in part to provide easy access to important essays in early American history and the history of ideas. But we have also selected with an eye to tracing through

Introduction

a twenty-year period the development of Max Savelle's liberal position. It is our conviction that these articles, when taken together, constitute a valuable discussion of the history of liberalism in America.

Moreover, we believe that the reader will find in these articles the humane and generous qualities and the zest for truth that have made Max Savelle so notable a scholar and teacher. Most of all, we offer these essays as a tribute to the man with whom our association has been a rich and an unforgettable experience.

JOHN VAN DE WETERING

PART I

Liberalism

IS LIBERALISM DEAD?

At last the Best of Artisans ... accorded to Man the function of a form not set apart, and a place in the middle of the world, and addressed him thus: 'I have given thee neither a fixed abode nor a form that is thine alone nor any function peculiar to thyself, Adam, to the end that, according to thy longing and according to thy judgment, thou mayest have and possess that abode, that form, and those functions which thou thyself shalt desire. The nature of all other things is limited and constrained within the bounds of law prescribed by me: thou, coerced by no necessity, shalt ordain for thyself the limits of thy nature in accordance with thine own free will, in whose hand I have placed thee. ... Thou shalt have the power to degenerate into the lower forms of life, which are animal; thou shalt have the power, out of thy soul's judgment, to be reborn into the higher forms of life, which are divine.' "[1]

Such were the terms in which Pico della Mirandola celebrated, toward the end of the fifteenth century, the peculiar quality of man, his intellectual, imaginative, and moral freedom, in the morning of the birthday of the modern liberal tradition.

[1] Giovanni Pico della Mirandola, "Of the Dignity of Man," trans. Elizabeth L. Forbes, *Journal of the History of Ideas,* III (1942), 347-354: p. 348.

Max Savelle

Almost exactly five hundred years later, in the year of the Christian era 1956, another observer of the nature and the qualities of man, B. F. Skinner, had this to say: "... science ultimately explains behaviour in terms of 'causes' or conditions which lie beyond the individual himself. As more and more causal relations are demonstrated, a practical corollary becomes difficult to resist: it should be possible to *produce* behaviour according to plan simply by arranging proper conditions."[2]

If Professor Skinner is correct in his dictum that "science ultimately explains" human behavior in terms of causal influences that originate outside the individual, then Pico's attribution of freedom and self-direction to the human mind was an illusion, and all the liberalisms that have been based upon that idea were false and invalid because based upon an illusion. And we, as historians of ideas, are now in a position to write the history of the birth, flowering, and death of liberalism, much as Arthur O. Lovejoy wrote the history of the idea of "the Great Chain of Being."

Liberalism, considered as a self-conscious ideology of human self-determination resting upon the assumption that the individual human intelligence is autonomous and that the progress of civilization derives from the use of this autonomous intelligence in the efforts of humanity to survive and live the good life, is a peculiarly western and modern phenomenon. The question before us is, is this peculiarly western phenomenon now a thing of the past, at one with the worship of Baal or the idea of the Great Chain of Being? There are a good many historians, political scientists, sociologists, anthropologists, psychologists, theologians, and philosophers of our generation who believe that it is either dead or dying.

John H. Schaar, for example, who is a political scientist, in a recent book has said that "The great historical movement, called

2 B. F. Skinner, "Freedom and the Control of Men," *The American Scholar*, XXV, No. 1 (Winter, 1955-56), pp. 47-65: p. 47.

Is Liberalism Dead?

variously the Age of Liberalism, or of Progress, or of Enlightenment, which began in the city-states of Renaissance Italy and rose to a brilliant zenith in the late eighteenth century, is now on the wane,"[3] and John H. Hallowell, an English historian, says:

> Liberalism is the product of a climate of opinion that came into existence with the Renaissance and Reformation. It is the political expression of an individualistic *Weltanschauung*. As a political ideology born of a particular historical period in a specific sociological environment it is subject, like all such systems of ideas, to development, decline, and death.... Liberalism required not only the existence of the concept of an autonomous individual but also an environment congenial to the exercise of individual autonomy. The values posited by liberalism would have been meaningless apart from an environment and institutions in which these values could find practical expression in everyday life.[4]

The great French Catholic philosopher Jacques Maritain celebrates what he calls "the vanishing victory of liberalism"[5] in the name of a return to the principle of authority and a set of values that are eternal and transcendent. Says he,

> With the triumph of rationalism and liberalism, i.e., of a philosophy of freedom which makes of each abstract individual and his opinions the source of all right and truth, *spiritual unity* has "gone west"; we have ourselves been able to experience the benefits of this dispersion.
> But this individualistic liberalism was palpably a purely *negative* energy; it lived by its opposite and because of it. Once the obstacle has fallen it lacks any support.[6]

Thomas P. Neill, of St. Louis University, also welcomes the decline of Liberalism, and attributes its failure and disappearance to its secularism and its divorce from the Christian ideal:

> Classical Liberalism [he says] believed in the worth and the dignity of the human person, a concept at the very core of Christian

---

[3] John H. Schaar, *Loyalty in America* (Berkeley, 1957), pp. 115-116.
[4] John H. Hallowell, *The Decline of Liberalism as an Ideology, with Particular Reference to German Politico-Legal Thought* (London, 1946), pp. 1-3.
[5] Jacques Maritain, *True Humanism* (New York, 1938), p. 51.
[6] *Ibid.*, pp. 151-152.

social thinking.... Its very theory of liberty is based upon the Christian theory of freedom as a faculty given to every man by his Creator.... But Liberalism changed these Christian ideas, sometimes weakening them, sometimes twisting them to serve different ends, sometimes perverting them entirely....

In reducing men to a collection of isolated atoms it stripped them of their supporting associations, and finally it left them standing naked before the State.... To the State, then, countless thousands began to turn for protection from the inhumanity of the Liberal regime.... Gradually the State took over additional functions,... and by 1914 a more or less complete form of socialism became the obvious not-far-distant goal.[7]

For Reinhold Niebuhr, one of the great Protestant theologians of our time, human freedom, such as it is, is only man's freedom inevitably to succumb to the impulses of original sin and to destroy himself by his own pride and arrogance. It is only by surrendering his purposes to those of God that man may find salvation; but in surrendering to God he surrenders his own freedom. As for the autonomous individual guided by a free intelligence, for Niebuhr no such creature exists:

If Protestantism represents the final heightening of the idea of individuality within terms of the Christian religion, the Renaissance is the real cradle of that very unchristian concept and reality: the autonomous individual.... The fact is that the Renaissance uses an idea which could have grown only on the soil of Christianity. It transplants this idea to the soil of classic rationalism to produce a new concept of individual autonomy, which is known in neither classicism nor Christianity.[8]

Arnold Toynbee, like Jacques Maritain and Reinhold Niebuhr, attributes the decline of western civilization in modern times to its secular, humanistic outlook, and says that the decline of the West

had begun at the moment when Western Man thanked not God, but himself that he was as different a being from his "medieval"

[7] Thomas P. Neill, *The Rise and Decline of Liberalism* (Milwaukee, 1953), pp. 302, 305, 306-307.

[8] Reinhold Niebuhr, *The Nature and Destiny of Man* (2 vols. London, 1941), I, 64-65.

predecessor as the Pharisee claimed to be from the publican in the parable.[9]

The implication of all this is clear; if these observers are right, liberalism, conceived as an ideology based upon the concept of a free and objective human intelligence influencing or directing human events, is a thing of the past.

II

Now, when the historian of ideas turns to the popular moods and intellectual events of his own time, he is confronted by a mass of evidence that seems to support the judgment of the observers just cited that the liberal ideology is of a day that is gone. It is admittedly difficult, of course, for any historian to see his own era objectively and in terms of a broad historical perspective. But many capable publicists of our time have called attention to various aspects of the contemporary outlook that seem to point to the end of the historic faith in the autonomous individual intelligence. Thus many commentators have remarked, for example, upon the major political event of our time, the emergence of the omnicompetent, monolithic state—an event that seems to have brought with it a progressive decline in the status of the individual, whether economic, political, social, or intellectual. Many writers such as Arthur A. Ekirch, Jr., have recorded the features of the "garrison state" and the "police state."[10] John Schaar, in his analysis of the changing concepts of loyalty since 1945, has shown the many ways in which the government of the United States has placed itself above the law in the enforcement of a new form of loyalty which he identifies with intellectual and political conformity. For example, he says,

[9] Arnold Toynbee, *A Study of History* (10 vols. London, 1935-1954), VIII, 114.
[10] Arthur A. Ekirch, Jr., *The Decline of American Liberalism* (New York, 1955), pp. 314-364.

[7]

The government violates more than the law. It assaults standards of decency and privacy basic to American mores.... Whoever doubts that this in fact has been done need but consult the records of the loyalty boards, the dossiers of the F.B.I. (so far as they are known), the testimony of attorneys defending loyalty cases, and the numerous statements of individuals who have been caught in the sticky web of alleged loyalty.[11]

Indeed, the extent to which the State has invaded and diminished the freedom of the individual, in what Jay Sikes calls "a gradual, subtle, at times imperceptible journey toward the elusive goal of total security,"[12] is grimly documented by the *Internal Security Manual, Revised,* just published by the United States government.[13]

Nor are the omniscience and the omnipotence of the State confined to the concerns of loyalty and security. It enters into a myriad of activities directed toward participation in the welfare and other private concerns of the individual, who is progressively swallowed up in the great Leviathan. And he who pays his income tax today may well speculate whether this great new feudal master to whom he pays his feudal dues is any less demanding, or he himself any less bound to property than the serfs and vassals of the thirteenth century.

It is a curious but significant fact in the history of liberalism, as Thomas Neill points out, that whereas the liberals of the nineteenth century fought for the protection of the individual against the State, those of the twentieth came to depend upon the State to defend society against the all-too-rugged individual as well as against the imponderable forces of history over which the individual, however free, had no control. Now, it is the State itself that they fear.

But the monolithic State has not imposed its will upon the

[11] Schaar, *op. cit.,* p. 173.

[12] Jay Sikes, "A Guide to Perfect Security," *The Nation,* Vol. 184, No. 14 (April 6, 1957), p. 298.

[13] *Internal Security Manual, Revised.* Compiled by Senator Alexander Wiley (Washington, 1957).

people against their wishes. On the contrary, it is the people who are the State; and the government, in the steady and progressive extension of its powers, apparently has actually obeyed the wishes of the people, rather than imposed its will upon them. As democracy—conceived here as the control of the machinery of government by the people—has become more and more of a reality, its mood has appeared to move progressively away from the liberalism—or individualism—of the nineteenth century toward a progressively more extensive and more effective collectivism in outlook. This is what Alan Valentine calls "The Age of Conformity." As he says,

> Democracy's deflection from the ultimate ends of freedom has been too gradual and too happily rationalized to be widely noticed. But each detour has left its sense of direction less acute. Since democratic government, in spite of all its troubles, is obviously preferable to current tyrannies, there has been little incentive to check the compass in democracy's ship of state.[14]

Walter Lippmann observes the same phenomenon in a slightly different way. In what he calls the "obscure revolution," the masses of the people—or a majority of them—have seized control of the new all-powerful state, with a consequent partial paralysis of the freedom of the individual and of dissident minorities. When this happened, the sense of the "public philosophy" was lost, and the state lost its liberal sense of direction. Lippmann thus finds himself, along with so many other erstwhile "liberals," now in a position that is essentially conservative in that it seeks to conserve—or preserve—the values of liberalism in a society that, in the name of equality and democracy, has abandoned them.[15]

The apparent fact to be noted by the historian of thought is that the masses of the people acquiesce in the growing power of the State in matters formerly considered within the area of the

---

14 Alan Valentine, *The Age of Conformity* (Chicago, 1954), p. 168.
15 Walter Lippmann, *Essays in the Public Philosophy* (Boston, 1955), p. 31, *et passim.*

[9]

individual's inviolable rights. The present generation of students, for example, apparently knows little or nothing of the freedom enjoyed by the individual two generations ago. Apparently, the young citizen does not enjoy freedom; he does not expect it; indeed, he would probably be frightened by the prospect of a return to a situation in which he might be expected to be both free and responsible. He accepts the reality of the diminished freedom of the individual as a matter of course.[16]

And so it appears to be with American society as a whole. Of course, there are protests by individuals and by such groups as the American Civil Liberties Union or the American Association of University Professors. But the weakness of the protest and the bad popular odor in which protesting organizations and individuals are held only emphasize the fact that the masses of the people acquiesce in the prevailing mood of conformity. This is, indeed, the "age of conformity," as Alan Valentine calls it.

Some may counter that such events as the Supreme Court's "desegregation decisions" and discouragement of censorship are indicative of a mood prevailing in most of the country against racial or other discriminations which demonstrates a trend toward a greater degree of liberalism. On second thought, however, it appears that the demand for equality of social treatment, which does exist, must be carefully distinguished from a demand for a greater freedom for intellectual, social, or political dissent, which does not—or which, at least, seems to be distinctly on the wane. In other words, the move toward an end of discrimination and an equality of social privileges may be interpreted as only a part of the larger mood toward mass conformity and not at all a movement in the direction of genuine liberalism.

Nor is it strange, on mature consideration, that it should be so. Historically, the dominant intellectual outlook of every society and every civilization—and this registers a score for the behavioralists—has, generally, appeared to be a sort of rationalization

[16] Cf. *The Nation*, Vol. 184, No. 10 (March 9, 1957), pp. 199-214.

of the economic, social, and political forms of that society. As Hallowell suggests, the liberalism of the five hundred years between 1450 and 1950 appears to have been a rationalization of the actual conditions that existed then—conditions in which the autonomous economic, social, and political individual was in fact —or could be—a reality. If this principle be sound, then it would seem to follow that as the economic, social, and political conditions change in the direction of collectivization, as they certainly appear to be doing, the prevailing intellectual outlook may be expected to move—as it appears to be moving—in the same direction—that is, toward a collectivization of intellectual life.

III

That the intellectual outlook of the mid-twentieth century is characterized, at least in part, by a rationalization of the mass mind and the "age of conformity" is clearly demonstrated by the appearance of a formidable body of thought that, for the purposes of this discussion, may be grouped under Karl Mannheim's phrase, "the science of human behavior."[17]

Mannheim, indeed, stands as the world-famous leader of this school of thought—or did, until his death in 1947. For in his nostalgic passion for an intellectual or psychological unity, or "consensus," comparable to that which he fancied prevailed in the age of feudalism and scholasticism, and in a desperate effort to reformulate and revive a decadent liberalism in the face of the collectivization of society, Mannheim conceived of a new type of "planned society" whose destiny would follow the lines of what he called "planning for freedom,"[18] which would rest upon a scientific "sociology of knowledge."[19] All thinking, in the last analysis,

17 Karl Mannheim, *Freedom, Power, and Democratic Planning* (New York, 1950), p. 179. See also Mannheim's *Man and Society in an Age of Reconstruction* (New York, 1940), *Ideology and Utopia* (New York, 1951), and *Diagnosis of Our Time* (New York, 1944).
18 Mannheim, *Man and Society*, Part V.
19 Mannheim, *Ideology and Utopia*, Part II.

[11]

is social thinking; all truth is relative to the time and the society that holds it to be true. Thought, therefore, is only partial, at best, and is constantly changing; no body of knowledge or thought has any long-term permanence.

Traditional liberalism, of course, which was for Mannheim a sort of intellectual "anarchy," is a thing of the past. For "Liberalism," he says, "has a disintegrative influence on culture in modern mass society,"[20] and "as a system, . . . is no longer applicable. . . . In the bewildering complexity of institutional pressures the individual no longer sees his way to meaningful contributions to the common end."[21]

Liberalism failed, says Mannheim, because it overlooked the powerful irrational urges in men. The "science of human behavior" is a science of the whole man; and it has now advanced to the point at which the individual can be shaped to preconceived specifications almost at will.

B. F. Skinner, an American psychologist, is more explicit than Mannheim. As already noted, he insists that "science ultimately explains behavior in terms of 'causes' or conditions which lie beyond the individual himself,"[22] and he puts into the mouth of the chief protagonist in his utopian novel *Walden Two* the declaration that, "I deny that freedom exists at all. I must deny it—or my program would be absurd. You can't have a science about a subject matter which hops capriciously about. Perhaps we can never prove that man isn't free; it's an assumption. But the increasing success of a science of behavior makes it more and more plausible."[23]

As for history, says the Behavioralist,

> In science, experiments are designed, checked, altered, repeated —but not in politics. Hence our extraordinary slow progress

[20] Mannheim, *Man and Society*, p. vii.
[21] Mannheim, *Freedom, Power, and Democratic Planning*, p. 177.
[22] B. F. Skinner, "Freedom and the Control of Man," *The American Scholar*, XXV, No. 1 (Winter, 1955-56), pp. 47-65: p. 47.
[23] B. F. Skinner, *Walden Two* (New York, 1948), p. 214.

toward a science of government. We have no real *cumulative* knowledge. History tells us nothing. That's the tragedy of the political reformer. He has nothing to work with but a spurious science of history. He has no real facts—no real laws. . . .[24]

Again, Leslie H. White, an anthropologist, discussing human culture in general in the light of the Behavioralist's doctrine, says that a man's philosophy "is merely the response of his neuro-sensory-muscular-glandular system to the streams of cultural stimuli impinging upon him from the outside."[25]

"Man is wholly at the mercy of external forces [says White], astronomic and geologic. . . ."[26] "To call upon science, the essence of which is acceptance of the principle of cause and effect and determinism, to support a philosophy of free will is fairly close to the height of absurdity."[27] Curiously enough, it is precisely science, the science of biology, that today presents the strongest evidence in support of that very philosophy, as we shall see.

These are examples of the sort of "scientific" thinking about man and society that may very well turn out to be the most characteristic thought of this generation. But there are many other writers who, in one way or another, take note of the same or similar phenomena—such, for example, are David Riesman's description of the "other-directed" person,[28] Erich Fromm's study of the conformist psychology of the mass mind,[29] and William Whyte's recent description of "the organization man."[30] The climate of opinion is clearly changing; the autonomous mind, the "free" individual, appears no longer to be the ideal of this generation; its ideal is the person who is "well-adjusted" to life in the crowd, and this ideal appears to be supported by the scientific authority of the "science of human behavior."

[24] *Ibid.*, p. 162.
[25] Leslie H. White, "Man's Control Over Civilization: An Anthropocentric Illusion," *Scientific Monthly*, LXVI (March, 1948), 235-247: p. 242n.
[26] *Ibid.*, LXVI, 246.
[27] *Ibid.*, LXVI, 240.
[28] David Riesman, *The Lonely Crowd* (New Haven, 1950).
[29] Erich Fromm, *Escape from Freedom* (New York, 1941).
[30] William H. Whyte, *The Organization Man* (New York, 1956).

The historian, especially the historian of ideas, simply may not ignore such a variety of testimony by so many perspicacious and distinguished observers, such a mass of factual data that characterize the situation in which he lives, and such an imposing corpus of systematic thought rationalizing the whole phenomenon. Certainly this mass of testimony, factual evidence, and systematic thought would seem to indicate, fairly conclusively, that the liberal ideology is approaching, if it has not actually reached, the end of its life cycle. And the historian of ideas might well conclude that in a brief, bright interlude between the end of the ten thousand years of history that preceded the year A.D. 1450 and the beginning of the ten thousand or more that began in the year A.D. 1950, but only in that half-millennium, man was, or thought he was, free.

To be sure, there have been many powerful counter-arguments presented in the interest of preserving the liberal ideology and of showing that, far from resting upon an illusion, the intellectual validity of the liberal concept of the intellectually autonomous individual is attested by the facts of history, by the logic of philosophy, and by science.

Bertrand Russell, for example, optimistically, if somewhat naively, attributes the diminution of individual liberty in the face of the steady extension of the power of the State to "the impoverishment of the world and to the decay of commerce due to economic nationalism," plus the fear that has arisen out of the danger of war. Let these problems be solved and liberalism will revive: "If we can indulge the hope that the danger of war will be averted by the creation of an international government, and the danger of starvation by modern technique and control of population, then it is also possible to hope that fear will cease to dominate us to the extent to which it does at the present." In that case, he says, "liberty may again be allowed to have its legitimate sphere."[31]

[31] Bertrand Russell, "Can the Liberal Survive?" *Saturday Review*, March 19, 1955, pp. 22, 35.

Is Liberalism Dead?

Albert Guérard, with a refreshing, Rousseauistic defiance of the advancing omnicompetent State and the mass mind that have again put men in chains, recognizes that ". . . the machine age has made the *isolated* individual almost obsolete,"[32] but he refuses to believe that the free individual is obsolete, for all that:

> I am different, because I am a man, and all men are different. . . . I have no desire *"d'épater le bourgeois,"* to horrify the rotarian. . . . My one hope is to induce free thought in others; and the only way in which this can be achieved is by keeping my own thought scrupulously free.[33]

Louis Hartz believes that liberalism will be saved from its own self-destroying "liberal absolutism" and take a new form in response to the new challenge of internationalism:[34]

> What is at stake is a new level of consciousness, a transcending of irrational Lockianism, in which an understanding of self and an understanding of others go hand in hand. . . . In any case, given the totalitarian nature of Russian socialism, the hope of the free world surely lies in the power for transcending itself inherent in the American tradition.[35]

Morris Cohen, liberal philosopher, in 1946 warned of the possible effect of the mass mind and the vogue of conformity upon science itself: ". . . it is possible that with the decline of liberalism and the gradual uniformity and standardization of ideas which modern machinery facilitates, we may choke that free intellectual variability which is the source of genuine progress in science."[36]

The history of modern times, says Cohen, conclusively documents the validity of the liberal outlook. The new liberalism, of course, must recognize the collective interest and limit the individual interest where necessary. Yet, having recognized the

[32] Albert Guérard, *Testament of a Liberal* (Cambridge, 1956), p. 171.
[33] *Ibid.*, p. xii.
[34] Louis Hartz, *The Liberal Tradition in America* (New York, 1955), pp. 13, 285, 287.
[35] *Ibid.*, pp. 308-309.
[36] Morris R. Cohen, *The Faith of a Liberal* (New York, 1946), p. 2.

limitations of the collective interest and the fact that the human mind operates on mechanistic, irrational, and rational levels and that all levels are bound together in an organic whole, Cohen returns again and again to the position that, within these given limitations, or perhaps at a fourth level above them, the human intelligence is and must be free, and that the individual is and must be autonomous.

Joseph Wood Krutch also presents a formidable historical and logical argument against the "behavioralist" outlook, and particularly that of B. F. Skinner.

Taking as his targets Skinner's "ignoble utopia,"[37] *Walden Two,* the growing belief among "Educators, sociologists, and lawmakers," that the individual is less and less capable of doing anything for himself, and that he is "limitlessly plastic,"[38] along with the assumption by the behavioralists that all thinking is nothing more than reaction to influences upon the individual from outside himself, Krutch insists that there is some area, however small, in every individual in which the individual may move as an "independent particle." Krutch rests much of his argument upon "the stubborn fact of consciousness,"[39] and draws heavily upon Julian Huxley, the English biologist, for scientific confirmation. He quotes Huxley to the effect that

> The impulses which travel up to the brain along the nerves are of an electrical nature and differ only in their time relations, such as their frequency, and in their intensity. But in the brain, these purely quantitative differences in electrical pattern are translated into wholly different qualities of sensation. The miracle of mind is that it can transmute quantity into quality. This property of mind is something given—it just is so. It cannot be explained; it can only be accepted.[40]

"In the course of evolution [says Krutch] the epiphenomenon

[37] Joseph Wood Krutch, *The Measure of Man* (Indianapolis, 1954), p. 58.
[38] *Ibid.,* p. 40.
[39] *Ibid.,* p. 115ff.
[40] Quoted by Krutch from Julian Huxley, *Evolution in Action* (New York, 1953), pp. 92-93.

consciousness . . . 'emerged' as a phenomenon in its own right."[41]

But Krutch does not rest his case entirely upon the epiphenomenon consciousness; for he believes that beyond and apart from both the material and the conscious is the human sense of mystery—what Freud called the "psyche"—which is not merely the creature of conditioning. And he warns that

> . . . if the so-called epiphenomena are actually something more, if the very ability to imagine that we may be something more than "products" is something new in the universe and something which corresponds to a reality, then we may be having our last chance to make something of it. We should think twice before we consent to dismiss the possibility from our minds. If we do not, we may never be able really to think again.[42]

Finally, Charles Frankel, another philosopher, rises to the defense of liberalism and refutes, to his own satisfaction, the arguments and the anti-liberal philosophies of history of Mannheim, Maritain, Toynbee, and Niebuhr.

> The great problem [he says] . . . is to reconstruct the liberal tradition to make it applicable to an age of technical specialization, bureaucratized power, and mass movements. . . . The revival of liberal hopes depends upon their being attached to specific programs and definite objectives. . . .
> For the revolution of modernity . . . has been a moral revolution of extraordinary scope, a radical alteration in what the human imagination is prepared to envisage and demand . . . it has set loose the restless vision of a world in which men might be liberated from age-old burdens, and come to set their own standards and govern their own lives.[43]

IV

Generally speaking, the arguments of these protesters against the fact and the rationalization of the mass mind rest upon logic— the logic of philosophy and of historical evidence. They are

[41] *Ibid.*, p. 134.
[42] *Ibid.*, p. 261.
[43] Charles Frankel, *The Case for Modern Man* (New York, 1955), pp. 205, 208-209.

logical arguments; but when in history has the logic of philosophy prevailed against the logic of events?

The strongest point in the pro-liberal argument, indeed, does now seem to rest, not upon logic, but upon the testimony of science—the science, that is, of biology. For there are certainly some impressive biological data tending to justify a reasonable doubt as to whether either Skinner's resounding "science insists" or White's "science of culture" will really stand the test of the historian's critical examination of the evidence. There are a number of biologists, for example, who see an organic freedom of the human intelligence that is the direct opposite of the position taken by the behavioralists.

Julian Huxley, the English biologist quoted by Krutch, speaks, as we have seen, of the human consciousness as a sort of epiphenomenon that "cannot be explained; it can only be accepted."

Hermann J. Muller, of Indiana University, a distinguished geneticist, in describing this phenomenon, says:

> As, through association and analysis, an increasingly coherent and serviceable formulation or representation of the world outside becomes built up out of the neuronic reaction-complexes, we become justified in speaking of intelligence. Only here, at last, does foresight make its debut in the operation of living things. Moreover, within this same neuronic reaction system, a representation of the individual himself, including his own associations, gradually takes its place. A speaking individual, in referring to this phenomenon, then uses the expression "consciousness" or some equivalent. . . .[44]
>
> And if the mindless gene has [finally] generated mind and foresight, and then advanced from the individual to the social mind, to what reaches may not we and our heirs, the incarnations of that social mind, be able, if we will, to carry consciously the conquests of life?[45]

N. J. Berrill, another biologist, is clear and unequivocal on the subject of the biological basis of individualism:

[44] Hermann J. Muller, "Life," in *Man's Right to Knowledge: Second Series: Present Knowledge and New Directions* (New York, 1956), pp. 19-33: p. 29.
[45] *Ibid.*, p. 33.

Is Liberalism Dead?

Human beings vary in every quality of the mind and spirit as well as in physique and appearance, physiology and longevity.... Individualism is a greater attribute of the human species than of any other kind of living organism and much of the hate so rampant in human relations stems from this essential diversity and our failure to accept and understand it.... Rather than force our children along the lines of standardized sociability, fostering the illusion that they are supposed to be a uniform product of a human assembly line, we should be teaching them that the juvenile passion to be average, normal and secure is a retreat from life....[46]

This scientific view is corroborated by Roger J. Williams, who is a chemist, and who assembles a mass of chemical, anatomical, and physiological data to show that

The existence in every human being of a vast array of attributes which are potentially measurable...makes quite tenable the hypothesis that *practically every human being is a deviate in some respects.*[47]

Obviously, the two sets of "scientific" evidence presented to us, the historians of ideas, are mutually contradictory. The "scientist of human behavior" asserts that humans are infinitely plastic, and that human thought is formed by influences outside the individual; the biologists and the chemists present apparently irrefutable evidence that every individual is different from every other biologically—which includes mentally—and cannot be otherwise. If the behavioralists are right, liberalism is unquestionably an untenable illusion, because based upon a scientific fallacy. If the biologists are right, it is not necessarily dead. It may die, of course, for it is permissible to suppose that this unique biological mechanism called the individual "consciousness" or "intelligence" may atrophy and wither away if it be not used and developed as one of the mechanisms of survival. If men acquiesce in the moods of the "age of conformity," and stop using their capacity to think critically, they may conceivably lose the capacity altogether, and

[46] N. J. Berrill, *Man's Emerging Mind* (New York, 1955), p. 247.
[47] Roger J. Williams, "Chemistry Makes the Man," *Saturday Review*, April 6, 1957, pp. 42-46: p. 43.

see it become, from disuse, like the vermiform appendix, a useless vestigial organ for a function that has disappeared. But there is no observable reason why this must happen.

VI

What we are dealing with here is, in the last analysis, the question of the role, real or imagined, of the autonomous human intelligence (within the limitations recognized above) in the course of human history.

The liberal historian insists that this role has been real and effective—indeed, that all history is but the record of the achievements and the errors of autonomous human minds at work, however influenced they may have been by their own irrational impulses and however conditioned by society. As Herbert J. Muller, historian and critic, puts it,

> History has no meaning, in the sense of a clear pattern or determinate plot; but it is not simply meaningless or pointless. It has no certain meaning because man is free to give it various possible meanings.
> His freedom is sharply limited, of course. Man has to choose within the conditions imposed by his biological structure, his natural environment, and his cultural heritage. . . . Still, at any moment he has a wide range of choice, and is willy-nilly making more history. . . .[48]

If the historian accepts the sociological-behavioralist position, then all written history down to our time is, as Henry Ford said, "the bunk." The behavioralist has little or no use for history, in any case; but should he find himself interested he would inevitably be faced with the task of writing it all over again in the terms of his own explanation of human behavior.

The behavioralists, from Mannheim onward, seem to be driven by a compelling desire for "order," for "unity," for "consensus." But the historian of ideas might be permitted to ask the specula-

---

[48] H. J. Muller, *The Uses of the Past* (New York, 1952), p. 73.

tive question, why must we have intellectual order, or consensus, in any case? He might recognize that the alternative is the intellectual "anarchy" that Mannheim so greatly abhorred, but what's wrong with that? He could certainly argue, with great plausibility, that it has been out of such intellectual anarchy, and especially in the liberal half-millennium, that many of the greatest achievements of human intelligence have come. The preponderant movement of ideas, institutions, and social and political events in our time certainly seems to be away from the liberal outlook and toward the "sociological" one. But it is still highly debatable whether this trend is either necessary or inevitable.

Indeed, even if the historian accepts the sociological-behavioralist point of view as to human nature and the nature of thought, he must still face the logical conclusion that since, in that view, all thought is relative to the time and place that produced it and, therefore, of only passing and local validity, the sociological-behavioralist point of view is itself such a product of society and, by the same token, doomed to disappear as society changes in the future, as it inevitably must.

On the other hand, there is at least some evidence to justify the historical critic in arguing that the liberal ideology of the autonomous mind, having, like science, come to stay, may be just the needed mechanism with which to avoid the loudly proclaimed decline of western civilization following the pattern of other civilizations. Toynbee himself has laid down the "laws" of the rise and decline of civilizations, and the chief law of decline appears to be marked by the arrival of the moment when a given society ceases to be an open society, in which new, intelligent responses to the challenges it faces are welcomed and put to use, and becomes a closed one, in which the ruling minority refuses to receive or even consider new ideas that may involve the loss of its own power. If this law of decline can be broken by the continued application of the liberal premium upon new ideas and responses to the challenges that face modern society, then decline may be

[21]

evaded; if, on the other hand, the liberal ideology is definitely suppressed in the interest of the behavioralists' "other-directed" thought and action, this civilization may well be standing upon the brink of the abyss.

Finally, if the historian adopts the point of view that the men of the western world may avoid the decline of western civilization by more and better use of the free intelligence, two things would seem to follow: first, that they may deliberately employ the behavioralists' technique of social conditioning through education to cultivate the use of the free individual intelligence, and second, they may—if they will—raise the average level of the quality of the free intelligence in individual men by resorting to the technique they use in improving their breeds of horses—by the technique, that is, of biological breeding. Whatever they do, the future of liberalism appears to depend upon what use men make of their biologically free minds.

PROLEGOMENA TO A HISTORY
OF LIBERALISM IN
EIGHTEENTH-CENTURY ANGLO-AMERICA

THE TERM *liberalism* is difficult to define. Yet liberalism, as a current of ideas and attitudes, has been a powerful force in the history of western society since the Renaissance. It has been a highly significant historical determinant. It has a history; and any historical phenomenon whose history may be written may be described and analyzed, if not precisely defined. Indeed, it must be, if its history is to be written at all.

For the purposes of this essay, the use of the term will follow the explanation by R. G. Collingwood in his preface to the English translation of Guido de Ruggiero's classic *History of European Liberalism.* Liberalism according to Ruggiero, says Collingwood,

> begins with the recognition that men, do what we will, are free; that a man's acts are his own, spring from his own personality, and cannot be coerced. . . . The aim of Liberalism is to assist the individual to discipline himself and achieve his own moral progress; renouncing the two opposite errors of forcing upon him a development for which he is inwardly unprepared, and leaving him alone, depriving him of that aid to progress which a political system, wisely designed and wisely administered, can give.[1]

[1] Guido de Ruggiero, *The History of European Liberalism,* trans. R. G. Collingwood (London, 1927), p. vii.

But liberalism is not confined to the area of politics. For the basic assumption as to the nature of man is to be observed, in the periods when it may be identified, in all the areas of human thought, whether social, economic, religious, literary, or philosophical, as well as in the political. Nor does it always express itself in exactly the same terms; the terms used and the mechanisms envisaged for the realization of the ideal change with the *Zeitgeist*. Thus, the romantic liberalism of the early nineteenth century is not the same as the laissez-faire liberalism of Social Darwinism, and neither of these is the same as the liberalism that brought into existence the welfare state. By the same token, none of these three is exactly the same as the rationalistic, natural-rights liberalism of the eighteenth century. The common denominator that binds them all together as liberalism is the aspiration for individual freedom, or, to use the eighteenth-century word, liberty.

He who would write a history of this intellectual phenomenon in Anglo-America during the early and middle decades of the eighteenth century must first survey the problem and the evidence. The words *liberal* and *liberalism* apparently did not appear in the language as nouns until shortly after the year 1800. Was there, nevertheless, in English colonial America a body of ideas which, taken together, may be recognized as liberalism, as it has been described? If so, where is it to be found? What sort of evidence is to be used in isolating and analyzing it? If there was such a historical phenomenon, what was its setting in, and its relevance to, the total picture of the time and the society in which it existed? It is the purpose of this essay to attempt some such preliminary survey.

I

The first task confronting the historian of American liberalism in the eighteenth century might well be an examination of the current of liberal ideas flowing from the mother country to the colonies in that period. For the Americans were in large measure —although not entirely—dependent upon England for component ideas and fashions in the formulation of their own culture-complex.

Roland Stromberg,[2] Caroline Robbins,[3] and others have described the currents of religious and political liberalism that were moving in England during the late seventeenth and the eighteenth centuries, and both authors have indicated some of the many instances and ways in which these currents branched out and flowed to America. Just how much influence the ideas of such men as Harrington, Sidney, Molesworth, Hutcheson, Clarke, or Tillotson—to say nothing of Locke—had upon the thinking of American political, intellectual, and religious leaders has never been precisely shown, and probably cannot be. Yet, that there was such an influence appears to be certain, since American writers often refer to their English mentors; they paraphrase English writings; many of the books and essays of the English liberals were brought to America, by gift or by purchase, and found their way into the libraries of individuals and of colleges; some, indeed, were republished, in whole or in part, on this side of the Atlantic.

In this body of English liberal thought, certain common and oft-recurring themes appear: the natural freedom, political equality, and rational nature of men; the doctrine of natural rights; the liberalization of the prerequisites for political participation; the liberalization of mercantilist economic regulation; the liberalization of education; a rationalism in religion that envisaged a freeing of the individual from what were regarded as

[2] Roland N. Stromberg, *Religious Liberalism in Eighteenth-Century England* (London, 1954).
[3] Caroline Robbins, *The Eighteenth-Century Commonwealthmen: Studies in the Transmission, Development and Circumstances of English Liberal Thought from the Restoration of Charles II until the War with the Thirteen Colonies* (Cambridge, Mass., 1959).

[25]

the superstitions and obscurantisms of ancient faiths; the principles and practices of religious toleration; freedom of speech and of the press; and so on.

II

A survey of the writings of American political thinkers of the eighteenth century discovers many echoes of the ideas of the English political liberals of the same era. To begin with, the words *liberty* and *liberties* literally stud the writings of the American publicists. Poets praised Liberty; her protagonists defended her; philosophers expounded her positive contributions to the promotion of human happiness:

> O Liberty, thou Goddess heavenly bright!
> Profuse of Bliss, and pregnant with Delight!
> Eternal Pleasures in thy Presence Reign,
> And smiling Plenty leads thy wanton Train.
> Eas'd of its Load, Subjection grows more light,
> And Poverty looks chearful in Thy Sight.
> Thou mak'st the gloomy Face of Nature gay,
> Giv'st Beauty to the Sun, and Pleasure to the Day.
> 'Tis Liberty that crowns Britannia's Isle
> And makes her barren Rocks and her bleak Mountains smile.[4]

Nor was the poet Portius a voice crying in a wilderness. Two decades earlier John Wise had proclaimed the liberty of the New England churches; and other libertarians, to the north and to the south of Portius, were singing the praises and expounding the ways of the goddess in every field of activity of the human intellect.

For Wise, the issue was ostensibly the freedom of the Congregational churches of New England to govern themselves. But Wise's disquisitions were essentially political, focussed upon the nature of government in general, which, in turn, rested upon the nature of man himself. For Man, says Wise, is endowed with an

[4] "Portius," *O Liberty, Thou Goddess Heavenly Bright* (New York, 1732), p. 1.

"original Liberty," that is stamped upon his nature, and "He that intrudes upon this Liberty, violates the Law of Nature."[5]

Wise appears to have been without significant influence upon the political thinkers of his own or succeeding generations. Yet the ideas that he expressed were echoed in the three decades following his death by American Whigs in practically all the continental colonies. In New York, for example, William Livingston, politician, philosopher, and poet, spoke the language of liberalism in the *Independent Reflector* on August 23, 1753:

> The Study of Human Nature will teach us, that Man in his original Structure and Constitution, was designed to act in a natural and moral Dependence on his Maker alone, and created solely for the Enjoyment of his own Happiness.... Thus Liberty of Action, however modified by human Policy, cannot in the Nature of Things be separated from his Existence. For by admitting the Rationality of Man, you necessarily suppose him a free Agent. And as no political Institutions can deprive him of his Reason, they cannot by any Means, destroy his native Privilege of acting freely.[6]

John Randolph, upon accepting the speakership of the Virginia House of Burgesses in 1736, defined the meaning of Parliamentary privileges and their relationship to liberty in these terms:

> Freedom of Speech is the very Essence of their Being, because, without it, nothing could be thoroly debated, nor could they be look'd upon as a Council; an Exemption from arrests, confirm'd by a Positive Law, otherwise their Counsels and Debates might be frequently interrupted, and their Body diminished by the Loss of its Members; a Protection for their Estates, to prevent all Occasions to withdraw them from the necessary Duty of their Attendance; a Power over their own Members, that they may be answerable to no other Jurisdiction for anything done in the House; and a sole Right of determining all Questions concerning their own Elections,

[5] John Wise, *A Vindication of the Government of the New England Churches* (Boston, 1717), p. 65.

[6] *The Independent Reflector* (New York), No. XXXIX (August 23, 1753), p. 156. I follow the attribution of articles in the *Independent Reflector* suggested by Dorothy R. Dillon, *The New York Triumvirate* (New York, 1949), pp. 34-35 n.

lest contrary Judgments, in the Courts of Law, might thwart or destroy Theirs.[7]

The rights of free government, as such men defined them, were to them sacrosanct and were to be defended by every means— even, if necessary, by resort to arms. This was the message of Jonathan Mayhew's famous sermon of 1750.[8] But Mayhew was not alone, for there were many others who would defend liberty, as a last resort, by the appeal to arms. Four years before Mayhew's pronouncement, for example, John Barnard had propounded the same idea in the election sermon for 1746:

> For one person alone to have the Government of a People in his hands, would be too great a Temptation. It tends to excite and draw forth the Pride of man, to make him unsufferably haughty; it gives him too much Liberty to exert [?] his Corruptions; and it encourages him to become a Tyrant and an oppressor, to dispense with Laws and break the most solemn oaths. To proceed so far in his unrighteous Practices, that his Subjects weary of the doctrine of passive obedience and non-resistance, are necessitated to plead their own cause and vindicate Their Rights by Measures which for a long time they were loth to make use of . . . [as in the time of King James II the English people] armed themselves in defence of their Religion and Liberties; the Consequence of which was his abdicating the Throne.[9]

The great objective of political institutions, indeed, was always, for these commentators, political liberty. In the last analysis, political liberties were an individual matter, which was closely identified with property and, therefore, taxation. Political institutions were created to defend and perpetuate the enjoyment of these liberties. There could be no compromise. Our poet-publicist, Portius, concluded that

> It is certain therefore, that a State or Colony cannot be too jealous of its Liberties, which, if once lost, are seldom or never recovered.

[7] H. R. McIlwaine, ed., *Journals of the House of Burgesses of Virginia, 1727-1734, 1736-1740* (Richmond, 1905-1915), VI, 242.

[8] Jonathan Mayhew, *Discourse on Unlimited Submission* (Boston, 1750).

[9] John Barnard, *The Presence of the Great God in the Assembly of Political Rules* (Boston, 1706), pp. 11-12.

The Preservation of Liberty is a Point equally nice with the Preservation of a Ladies Chastity; the first Assaults are to be repell'd with the utmost Fortitude. A Maidenhead, a Fort, or a Constitution, that begins to capitulate, will soon surrender. If the Outworks are once given up, the Citadel cannot be long maintained.[10]

III

But political liberalism was only one form of the expression of liberal thought. Liberty was thought to be a condition of economic and social life, also. For the economic theorists, the ownership of property was a natural right. It followed that the free use of property was also a natural right. This was the economic basis of the idea of voluntary self-taxation that had come to America almost with the first colonists. This doctrine was expounded thus by "Philalethes," in 1744:

As Reason tells us, all are born thus naturally equal, i.e., with an equal Right to their Persons; so also with an equal Right to their Preservation; and therefore to such Things as Nature affords for their Subsistence. . . . And every Man having a Property in his own Person, the Labour of his Body and the Work of his Hands are properly his own, to which no one has the Right but himself; it will therefore follow that when he removes any Thing out of the State that Nature has provided and left it in, he has mixed his Labour with it and joined something to it that is his own, and thereby makes it his Property. . . . Thus every Man having a natural Right to . . . his own Person and his own Actions and Labour, which we call Property, it certainly follows, that no Man can have a Right to the Person or Property of another: And if every Man has a right to his Person and Property; he has also a Right to defend them, and a Right to all the necessary Means of Defence, and so has a Right of punishing all Insults upon his Person and Property.[11]

The acceptance of the right of private property alone, however,

---

[10] "Portius," *op. cit.*, pp. 1-2.
[11] Elisha Williams ("Philalethes," pseud.), *The Essential Rights and Liberties of Protestants. A Seasonable Plea for the Liberty of Conscience, and the Right of Private Judgment, in Matters of Religion, without any Control from Human Authority*, as quoted in Alice M. Baldwin, *The New England Clergy and the American Revolution* (Durham, 1928), p. 65.

need not necessarily be considered characteristic only of the liberal outlook, because it was universally accepted by liberals and conservatives alike. It was in the liberals' demands for the free use of property and in their challenges to certain forms of mercantilist economic restriction that some of the American economic thinkers betrayed a mood that may be called liberal. Thus Jeremiah Dummer's *Defence of the New-England Charters* should be classed among liberal political and economic writings, since it pleaded eloquently for the economic autonomy of the colonies in the midst of an empire that was regulated by policies that were highly mercantilistic in spirit and execution. With Dummer, liberty, especially the economic liberty of the colonies, was not merely a right; it was also a mechanism for achieving prosperity. England's own wealth, he maintained, had derived from the prosperity of the colonies, whose contributions to English prosperity would hardly have been possible without the high degree of economic liberty they had enjoyed. It followed, according to Dummer, that it is a natural condition of the colonies that they should make laws for their own economic self-direction: "Every Country has Circumstances peculiar to it self in Respect of its Soil, Situation, Inhabitants and Commerce, to all which, convenient Laws must, with the nicest Care and Judgment, be adapted."[12] England had laws proper to itself; let the Anglo-Americans be free to make laws expedient to their needs and circumstances.

Dummer's doctrine of colonial freedom for economic self-direction was echoed by Benjamin Franklin. As Dummer had said, there was no danger that a free commerce of the colonies in manufactured articles would compete with that of the mother country, since the colonies were not, and probably would never be, industrial societies. Franklin wrote to David Hume in 1760 that freedom of commerce would be to "the *interest of humanity,*

[12] Jeremiah Dummer, *A Defence of the New-England Charters* (Boston, 1721), p. 33.

or common good of mankind,"[13] and to Dupont de Nemours, in 1767,

> We [Englishmen] are so far from conceiving that what is best for mankind, or even for Europe in general, may be best for us, that we are even studying to establish and extend a separate interest of Britain, to the prejudice of even Ireland and our colonies. . . . It is from your philosophy [i.e., the physiocratic doctrine of freedom of commerce] that the maxims of a contrary and more happy conduct are to be drawn, which I therefore sincerely wish may grow and increase till it becomes the governing philosophy of the human species, as it must be that of superior beings in better worlds.[14]

Here is enlightened self-interest again; here, also, is the universalism of the principles of liberty. But economic liberalism was individual as well as colonial or provincial in its outlook. Anglo-America was the land of the self-made man. Nowhere, probably, were the contemporary doctrines of enlightened self-interest and of the self-made man more clearly or more extensively articulated than in eighteenth-century Anglo-America.

It would be beside the point to note that Benjamin Franklin and his contemporaries were not yet entirely free of certain of the predispositions of mercantilism. The point is that there was much of the ideology of economic freedom in the air, both freedom for the individual and freedom for the colonial societies.

Economic individualism and colonial economic self-determinism were closely akin to social individualism and colonial sociological self-determinism. If men and societies were naturally free economically, they were also naturally free socially. The Anglo-American experience had produced a society—or set of societies —of which internal social mobility, both of the person and of social status, was characteristic. After all, the population of Anglo-America was highly conglomerate, composed of persons

---

[13] *The Writings of Benjamin Franklin*, collected and edited by Albert Henry Smyth (New York and London, 1905-1907), IV, 83.
[14] *Ibid.*, V, 155-156.

who had moved from all the countries of western Europe, from Africa, and even from Latin America. And Anglo-America was already coming to be known as an asylum where the unfortunate and the oppressed of Europe might find freedom, refuge from the Old World's restraints upon the human spirit, and a future illumined by infinite progress. Anglo-America,

> Where the sick Stranger joys to find a Home,
> Where casual Ill, maim'd Labor, freely come
> Those worn with Age, Infirmity or Care,
> Find Rest, Relief, and Health returning fair.
> There too the Walls of rising Schools ascend,
> For Publick Spirit still is Learning's Friend,
> Where Science, Virtue, sown with liberal Hand,
> In future Patriots shall inspire the Land.[15]

This doctrine of personal mobility was written clearly into the laws of naturalization, which liberalized the procedures for acquiring citizenship by non-English immigrants.

Inevitably the belief in the freedom of the individual in society ran head-on into the institution of slavery, and the Anglo-Americans had to face it sooner or later. The doom of slavery was inherent in the rationalist's doctrine of human freedom and equality of rights in a state of nature; it was logically imperative from the Quaker's religious doctrine of individual spiritual worth. As John Woolman put it, "though we made slaves of the Negroes and the Turks made slaves of the Christians, I believed that liberty was the natural right of all men equally...."[16]

But Woolman had been poignantly anticipated by that hoary old secular Puritan, the morning-star of the anti-slavery movement in Anglo-America, Samuel Sewall:

> Forasmuch as Liberty is in real value next unto Life; None ought to part with it themselves, or deprive others of it, but upon the most mature Consideration.... It is most certain that all Men, as they are the Sons of Adam, are Co-heirs, and have equal Right

---

[15] *Poor Richard Improved*, 1752, "April."
[16] John Woolman, *Journal*, ed. Janet Whitney (Chicago, 1950), p. 47.

unto Liberty, and all other outward comforts of Life. . . . So that Originally, and Naturally, there is no such thing as Slavery.[17]

And Sewall was followed by many others.

Obviously, the whole anti-slavery movement of the eighteenth century must be regarded as a manifestation of one of the essential attitudes of liberalism.

IV

Libertarian currents were moving in religion also. Apart from the fact that the English colonies were the receptacle of many varieties of Christians and some Jews living peaceably together, despite the presence on the statute books of laws limiting the religious freedom of some groups and their members, and apart from the fact that the bulk of the citizens of the colonies were still of an orthodox mood in their own faiths, there were moving in the land two currents of religious thought that must be called liberal. One was a combination of naturalism and rationalism (i.e., eighteenth-century empiricism) in theology itself; the other was a body of conscious thinking upon the nature and the desirability of religious toleration.

In the first case, the liberal theologians held with the political liberals that man is naturally endowed with reason, the function of which is the guidance of the individual in his choices between right and wrong. From this it followed that if men were to find the good life in religion in the light of reason, they both had a responsibility to use their reason—or intelligence—and had to be left free to do so. By the same token, any church, which was a congregation of like-minded believers, had to be left free to direct its own destinies, both as to theology and as to the selection of its own leadership.

It was this last point that had stirred John Wise to irony and eloquence early in the century. The churches of New England,

[17] Samuel Sewall, *The Selling of Joseph*, rptd. in George H. Moore, *Notes on the History of Slavery in Massachusetts* (New York, 1866), pp. 83-87.

he thought, could never accept the proposal that pastors be nominated for them by church councils. Such a proposal would be like having a man's wife picked out for him. It would not only usurp the sovereign jurisdiction of the church over its own freedom and liberties, but also the

> conjugal and secret Powers of Christs Virgin and widow Churches. That it seems to me very advisable [he says] (if this Proposal may stand for a sound Precept) that forth-with another Office be erected, and put into the hands and under the Government of a few men, exactly skilled in Phisiognamy, and deeply studied in the Sympathies and Antipathies of Humane Nature, with an absolute superintending Power to Controul and direct all Wooers in their choice for the Marriage Bed; for that there is many a fond Lover who has betrayed the glory of Wedlock, by making an unwise and unfortunate choice; and why may not particular Beds be over-Ruled as well as particular Churches?[18]

If some superior government could usurp the right of the church to elect its own pastor, why should not the state appoint a *censor familias* to take from the individual the function of choosing his own bed-mate?

But the logical implications of this position led straight to individual sovereignty in matters of belief. If man was naturally endowed with reason, as Wise had said, it was his responsibility to use it—and without external restraint; it was this way that lay advancement to enlightenment.

In Charles Chauncy, the injunction to the free exercise of reason was clear: Man is "an *intelligent moral agent*; having within himself an *ability* and *freedom* to will, as well as to *do*, in opposition to necessity from any extraneous cause whatever."[19]

Samuel Quincy expressed a similar advocacy of freedom of the mind in religion:

> Christianity is then a rational Religion, and those who deny it

[18] John Wise, *The Churches Quarrel Espoused* (New York, 1713), pp. 89-90.
[19] Charles Chauncy, *The Benevolence of the Deity, Fairly and Impartially Considered* (Boston, 1784), title page. (This work seems to have been formulated in Chauncy's mind, if not actually written, in the 1750's.)

can, or ought to be maintained upon rational Principles, do in Effect give it up. For is not reason the only Faculty of the Soul that God has given us, to render us capable of Religion: And would Men persuade us to lay it aside, in order to become more religious? A Monstrous Absurdity! 'Tis true, Reason is fallible, weak, and liable to be imposed on: But still it is the only Guide we have to direct us in our Searches after Truth; for without it we could neither distinguish Good from Evil, nor Truth from Falsehood, and might as well embrace a false Opinion, as a right one; and could be no more accountable to our Maker for the one, than for the other.[20]

This sort of religious liberalism meant a freeing of the religious mind from ignorance, from the binding inhibitions of myths and superstitions, and from what was thought to be an irrational belief in miracles; it meant, also, a rejection of the concept of God as a stern and inflexible Creator who would bind his creatures to hell forever under an iron law of sin and predestination. It involved a total freeing of the religious mind, in the name of reason, of individual religious sovereignty and responsibility, and of an humanitarian faith in the capacity of the free human mind to choose between good and evil. It involved, further, the autonomy of corporate religious societies, or churches, in the determination of their theology and in their religious behavior.

This faith in, and dependence upon, individual reason implied the necessity for individual freedom of conscience and the basic principles of religious toleration. It was probably true that, as Franklin later observed, the English colonies in America enjoyed and practiced a greater degree of religious toleration than any other society in the world, greater even than England itself.[21]

But this was the practical situation. How was it rationalized by the liberals who believed in religious toleration as a matter of principle? To begin with, the habit of lay critical comment upon religion and religious practices, if not universally encouraged, was increasingly widespread and intellectually respectable.

[20] Samuel Quincy, *Twenty Sermons* ... (Boston, 1750), p. 12.
[21] *Writings of Benjamin Franklin*, ed. Smyth, V, 399-405.

Max Savelle

A good example of such criticism is to be seen in one of the satirical essays in *The Independent Reflector:*

> The Transubstantiation of the Elements into Flesh and Blood, by the Mouth of a Romanist Priest, [is] equally possible with the Transmutation of Sinners and Numskulls into Saints and Scholars, by the Hands of a Protestant Priest; ... Religion doth not consist in black Coats, or black Cassocks, in Hats ros'd or unros'd, in Bands or Surplices, in cant Phrases or demure Looks, but in loving God and keeping his Commandments; ... there is more Iniquity committed under the Rose, than is repented of under the Gallows; ... in one Sense a black Petticoat is like charity, often *covering a Multitude of Sins.*[22]

But the essential principle was the principle of the validity of private judgment. Archibald Kennedy, of New York, addressed his son thus:

> I allow you Freedom of Conscience, to think, and judge for yourself; and I likewise allow you Freedom, if not entirely from all Manner or Influence, yet from the Dominion of human authority, in thinking and judging for yourself. I am so much for Liberty in these Matters that concerns us, as reasonable Beings, that I must recommend to you, on the other Hand, a third Sort of Freedom; that is, a Freedom from Pride, Singularity, and the Spirit of Contradiction. ... As for my own Part, I have no Notion, of Religion's passing by Descent, or Inheritance, as Estates do; nor am I for craming my Religion down my child's throat. This, in my humble Opinion, would be a species of Persecution; if he has good sense, and [is] capable of judging, let him choose.[23]

The argument for religious toleration presented by Benjamin Franklin was based upon the nature of man and the relativity of all human knowledge. Incidentally, too, he recognized the impact upon the thinking of the individual of the sociological forces at work about him:

> When the natural weakness and imperfection of human under-

[22] *The Independent Reflector* (New York), No. XLVI (Thursday, October 11, 1753), p. 187.
[23] Archibald Kennedy, *A Speech Said to Have Been Delivered Some Time Before the Close of the Late Session, by a Member Dissenting from the Church* (New York, 1755), pp. 28-29.

standing is considered, the unfavorable influence of education, custom, books, and company upon our ways of thinking, I imagine a man must have a good deal of vanity who believes, and a good deal of boldness who affirms, that all the doctrines he holds are true, and all he rejects are false. And perhaps the same may be justly said of every sect, church, and society of men, when they assume to themselves that infallibility, which they deny to the Pope and councils.

But, since it is no more in a man's power to *think* than to *look* like another, methinks that all that should be expected of me is, to keep my mind open to conviction, to hear patiently, and examine attentively, whatever is offered to me for that end.[24]

Religion must be left free, because men naturally differed and because there appeared to be no such thing as absolute truth. But this was still a negative sort of religious toleration. It was the Quakers who made of religious toleration a positive philosophy. For the logic of the Quaker doctrine of the inner voice led straight to the conclusion that if, when another speaks, it is the voice of God speaking through him, one does not just suffer him to speak: one listens to what he has to say. One does not merely tolerate God; one welcomes instruction from him.

Religious toleration thus came to be more than just suffering another to speak; it began to mean, by implication at least, an attitude of listening to, and learning from, what another has to say. This attitude was particularly characteristic of the secular sciences, in which the scientists took great satisfaction in learning from one another. But even in religion, the liberal positions, whether those of the Revolutionists or those of the Quakers, centered about the idea that progress toward truth depended upon both freedom of expression and a willingness to be influenced by it.

V

The first half of the eighteenth century was a period in which the liberal attitude also manifested itself in the rapid growth and

24 *Writings of Benjamin Franklin,* ed. Smyth, II, 214-215.

repeated articulation of the principle of freedom of the press. The young Benjamin Franklin had met this problem in the flesh, as it were, when his brother James had been jailed in 1722 by the irate Massachusetts authorities who were angered by James's criticism, in the *New England Courant,* of their failure to apprehend a pirate vessel thought to be operating off the coast. Benjamin, publishing the paper in his brother's place, printed, as the eighth of his "Silence Dogood" papers, an essay on Freedom of Speech and Communication (one of "Cato's Letters") that he copied *in extenso* from the *London Journal,* the burden of which was,

> Without Freedom of Thought, there can be no such thing as Wisdom; and no such thing as publick Liberty, without Freedom of Speech; which is the Right of every Man, so far as by it, he does not hurt or controul the Right of another: And this is the only Check it ought to suffer, and the only Bounds it ought to know.[25]

A few years later, now in Philadelphia, in his "Apology for Printers," published in the *Pennsylvania Gazette* of June 10, 1731, he put the principle into his own words:

> 1. That the Opinions of Men are almost as various as their Faces; an Observation general enough to become a common Proverb, *So many Men so many Minds....*
> 5. Printers are educated in the Belief, that when Men differ in Opinion, both Sides ought equally to have the Advantage of being heard by the Publick; and that when Truth and Error have fair Play, the former is always an overmatch for the latter: Hence they chearfully serve all contending Writers that pay them well, without regarding on which side they are of the Question in Dispute....
> 8. That if all Printers were determin'd not to print any thing till they were sure it would offend no body, there would be very little printed.[26]

Franklin was to re-state the principle of freedom of the press

---

[25] *The Papers of Benjamin Franklin,* ed. Leonard W. Labaree and Whitfield J. Bell, Jr. (New Haven, 1959), I (Jan. 6, 1706, through Dec. 31, 1764), 27.
[26] *Ibid.,* I, 194-195.

again and again in the course of his long life. But there were many who shared Franklin's convictions on this subject.

The most famous incident in the history of the freedom of the press in the colonies was, of course, the case of John Peter Zenger; and the most famous articulation of the principle was the address of Andrew Hamilton, Zenger's counsel, to the jury in that case. Hamilton linked the freedom of the press with the right of the citizen to complain against an arbitrary government:

> [The right to complain against an arbitrary government] is a right which all freemen claim, that they are entitled to complain when they are hurt. . . .

We have freedom to criticize religion in New York, said Hamilton, but not freedom to criticize the government:

> From which I think it is pretty clear, that in New-York a man may make very free with his God, but he must take special care what he says of his governor. The loss of liberty to a generous mind [he continues], is worse than death; . . . the man, who loves his country prefers its liberty to all other considerations, well knowing that without liberty life is a misery. . . .
> The question before the Court and you gentlemen of the jury, is not of small or private concern. It is not the cause of a poor printer nor of New-York alone, which you are now trying: No! It may in its consequence affect every free man that lives under a British government on the main of America. It is the best cause. It is the cause of liberty! . . . [It is] that to which nature and the laws of our country have given us a right—the liberty of both exposing and opposing arbitrary powers (in these parts of the world at least) by speaking and writing truth.[27]

It has been argued, probably correctly, that the acquittal of Zenger by the jury had no perceptible influence, either upon the law of libel or upon court practice. The point here is that the idea of freedom of the press was widely accepted, and was expressed, in one way or another, by an increasing number of thinkers on the subject. William Smith of New York, for

---

[27] Vincent Buranelli, ed., *The Trial of Peter Zenger* (New York, 1957), 118. 122-123, 128, 131.

example, published a lengthy and penetrating essay on liberty of the press—and the responsibility that must accompany it—in *The Independent Reflector* in 1753, in terms that echo the language of Andrew Hamilton in the Zenger trial:

> The Liberty of complaining, of carrying that complaint to the Throne itself, and of breathing the Sighs of an afflicted, oppressed Nation, has too great a Tendency to produce a Revolution to be suffered in despotic Government....
> No Nation in *Europe,* is more jealous of the *Liberty of the Press* than the *English,* nor is there a People, among whom it is so grossly abused.... We are so besotted with the Love of Liberty, that running into Extreams, we even tolerate those things which naturally tend to its Subversion....[28]

The idea of the freedom of the press was clearly present in the intellectual atmosphere. What was it in the sociological situation in the colonies that made this principle welcome in the colonial mind? Andrew Hamilton was given the freedom of the city of New York for "his learned and generous defence of the rights of mankind, and the liberty of mankind, and the liberty of the press...."[29] There was evidently something in the situation of New York society that caused the city fathers to identify Zenger with themselves, and to recognize his cause as, somehow, not only their own but also that of all mankind.

VI

The same moods are to be observed in the thinking of a number of intellectual leaders on the subject of education. This was a period when education itself was changing, in the direction of greater secularization and greater practical functionalism, as Benjamin Franklin put it in a famous book.[30]

[28] *The Independent Reflector,* No. XL (Thursday, August 30, 1753), pp. 160-161. For this attribution, see *supra,* fn. 7. Cf. Leonard W. Levy, "Did the Zenger Case Really Matter?" *William and Mary Quarterly,* 3d Ser., XVII (Jan. 1960), 35-50.

[29] Buranelli, ed., *The Trial of Peter Zenger,* p. 133.

[30] Benjamin Franklin, *Proposals Relating to the Education of Youth in Pennsylvania* (Philadelphia, 1749), p. 11.

Actually, the American colonies were societies in the midst of profound social change. Economic and social conditions were highly fluid, and the individual not only could but did move up or down the economic or social scale according to his abilities. Education was one of the mechanisms for moving upward on the scale. At the same time, Franklin's proposals appear to have have been a response to the needs of society for the sort of education that would prepare young people for the task of finding the good life in a society in flux. The function of education was that of aiding and abetting social change.[31]

This is to be seen, for example, in the emphasis that was placed upon the idea of education for citizenship. William Smith, future provost of the College of Philadelphia, said, "The Knowledge of what tends neither directly nor indirectly to make better Men and better Citizens, is but a Knowledge of Trifles; it is not Learning, but a specious and ingenious sort of Idleness."[32] The same general idea of education for citizenship was also expressed by Archibald Kennedy of New York:

> The Intention and Design of Seminaries, in every Country governed by Laws, are to form the Minds of Youth, to Virtue, and to make them useful Members of the Society, in whatever Station may be allotted to them, in Conformity to the Law of the Land. . . . In Countries, where Liberty prevails, and where the Road is left open for the Son of the weariest Plebeian to arrive at the highest Pitch of Honors and Preferments, there never will be wanting great Emulation, and of Course great men.[33]

In the minds of these educational leaders, education was an instrument for finding the good life in the free society. For the individual it included the freeing of the mind from ignorance

[31] Cf. Bernard Bailyn, "Education in the Colonies: Opportunities and Needs for Study," a paper presented at a Conference on Early American Education sponsored by the Institute of Early American History and Culture, September 17, 1959.

[32] William Smith, *A General Idea of the College of Mirania* (New York, 1753), p. 10.

[33] Archibald Kennedy, *A Speech Said to have been delivered* . . . (New York, 1755), pp. 13-14.

and superstition, the acquisition of knowledge of nature and of men, a deepening of the understanding, and an encouragement of invention—or opportunity—in industry and the arts. Education in these terms was thought of as an instrument for the liberalization of the life of the mind.

VII

All the expressions thus far noticed, in the realms of thought about politics, economic and social life, religion, the press, and education revolve, each in its own orbit, about the general concept of liberty and of its values for society and the individual. They might be said to move by gradations upward from discussions of freedom of action in the areas of politics or of economic and social life, through the thinking that was directed toward religious liberty, to a concern with freedom of communication in the press and in the halls of education. The apex of the structure was reached in the examination of the nature and the value of the freedom of the mind *per se*. The keynote here is sounded by Jonathan Mayhew:

> Free examination, weighing arguments for and against, with impartiality, is the way to find the truth. Who imagines that free inquiry into philosophical [i.e., scientific] subjects has any tendency to lead men into a wrong idea of the natural world? ... And it is in all respects as unprobable that free inquiry into religious subjects should lead us into wrong notions concerning the moral world. ... Error and ignorance fly from the light, like the owl and bat; but truth and honesty, like the noble eagle, face to the sun. ...

As for the right of every man to search for truth,

> This right was given them by God, and nature, and the gospel of Christ; and no man has a right to deprive another of it, under a notion that he will make an ill use of it, and fall into erroneous opinions.[34]

[34] Jonathan Mayhew, *Two Objections to the Right and Duty of Free Inquiry and Private Judgment Answered.* Second ed. (Boston, 1830), pp. 2, 3, 5.

Prolegomena to a History of Liberalism

By no one, probably, was the principle of the free exchange of ideas more eloquently stated than by John Randolph, upon the occasion of his acceptance of the speakership of the Virginia House of Burgesses in 1734:

> Then we shall hear one another patiently, put the Weight of every Man's Reason in the Ballance against our own, and at last form a Judgment on the whole matter; which, if not the wisest, . . . will be honest and commendable. . . . And, however Mankind may be provoked, by being thwarted with the Sentiments of other Men, a Variety of Opinions is not only absolutely necessary to our Natures, but is likewise of all Things the most useful; since if all Men were of one Mind, there would be no need of Councils; no Subject for Learning and Eloquence, the Mind would want its proper exercise, and without it, like the Body, would lose its natural Strength from a Habit of Sloth and Idleness. Truth itself will receive an Addition of Strength by being opposed, and can never be in Danger of Suffering by the Test of Arguement.[35]

Americans were conscious of the fact that in the British Empire, and especially in their part of it, there was a greater degree of freedom of expression than in any other society in the world. Jonathan Mayhew, again, in the preface to his famous sermon of 1750 on unlimited submission, gloried in this fact:

> GOD be thanked, one may, in any part of the *British* dominions, speak freely (if a decent regard be paid to those in authority) both of government and religion; and even give some broad hints, that he is engaged on the side of Liberty, the BIBLE and Common Sense, in opposition to Tyranny, PRIEST-CRAFT and Nonsense, without being in danger either of the *Bastile* or the *Inquisition*.[36]

For all these eighteenth-century liberals the mind was, by its very nature, free. The mind is an instrument for finding truth; it can operate effectively only in freedom; anything that interferes with this freedom is, by definition, an interference with human nature and with the march of progress.

[35] H. R. McIlwaine, ed., *Journals of the House of Burgesses of Virginia, 1727-1734, 1736-1740* (Richmond, 1905-1915), VI, 175-176.
[36] Jonathan Mayhew, *Discourse on Unlimited Submission*, p. v.

Max Savelle

CONCLUSION

From this preliminary survey of the problem and a sketchy sampling of the extant mass of evidence, the following conclusions (or hypotheses) may be suggested:

First, there was a recognizable corpus of ideas and attitudes in Anglo-America in the eighteenth century that may be identified as liberalism, as defined above. This liberalism expressed itself clearly and forcibly in, if it did not actually dominate, the thinking that was going on about politics, economic and social life, religion, the press, education, and intellectual life generally. The major source of the liberal ideas expressed seems to have been the thinking of the English liberals of the late Stuart and early Hanoverian periods. But American liberal expression was not a mere echo of English thought; on the contrary, American liberal ideas were responses to American situations, and while there were many English ideas expressed, these ideas appeared to have been reformulated to fit into the American context. Besides which, there appear to have been numerous cases in which the Americans were more vigorous than the English Whigs, both in the expression of old ideas and in the creation of new ones.

As in all societies, however, the liberal consensus was neither universal nor unanimous. On the contrary, Conservatism, the antithesis of Liberalism, was also a powerful force in the course of intellectual and practical events.[37] It would be misleading, however, to label any individual a liberal or a conservative in the sense that all his ideas were liberal or that all were conservative. For it is difficult to discover a single intellectual leader in eighteenth-century colonial society who did not, at one time and another, give expression to both liberal ideas and conservative ones. The problem for the intellectual historian is to isolate the ideas, as it were, from the men who held them and consider the ideas as phenomena in themselves, each with its own history.

[37] See Leonard W. Labaree, *Conservatism in Early American History* (New York, 1948).

Prolegomena to a History of Liberalism

The history of ideas becomes, thus, a true history of ideas, and not of men. Considered in this light, it is evident that the liberal ideas enumerated above did have a very active and widespread existence in Anglo-America.

The liberal ideology centered about the concept of liberty, which is to be understood as freedom of economic, social, or political action, freedom of religious belief, freedom of the press, and freedom of the intellect. There was hardly a systematic philosophy of liberalism *per se*, as, say, John Stuart Mill's thought may be said to have been a systematic philosophy of liberalism. Yet, there was clearly a body of opinion, or a consensus, or a widely accepted attitude that favored and promoted liberty in this sense and in all these areas of thought. In the history of liberalism this body of opinion, this ideology, may be characterized as rationalistic liberalism as distinguished from the romantic or laissez-faire liberalism of the nineteenth century.

It is probably safe to say that there was more social change going on in America than in England; America was a new and highly dynamic society; English society was relatively old, and, in this period, relatively static. Franklin's earliest pleas for freedom of the press were responses to actual, *de facto* situations, as was Andrew Hamilton's defense of Peter Zenger. So were the liberal pronouncements of Sir John Randolph, Lewis Morris, Jr., Archibald Kennedy, Samuel Davies, and a host of others. American society was changing in the course of its growth, and it was hammering out the ideas with which to rationalize its enlightened self-interest upon the anvil of actual, day-by-day experience and the actual, substantial needs of a society in the midst of rapid change and development.

It is not enough, however, to record that society was changing. It is to be assumed that to produce liberal thought the changes going on in society must be such as to make the ideal of freedom a desirable one. It might be illuminating to draw a comparison between the eighteenth century and the twentieth, when social change appears to be moving toward a lessening of individual liberty, and to examine twentieth-century thinking in this light. In any case, the nature of the social changes going on in eighteenth-century Anglo-America is one of the problems the historian of liberalism in that period must face. On the assumption that a significant portion of the social change going on was of a liberal sort, the liberal ideology seems to have been the ideology of this sort of social change,—as contrasted, say, with conservatism, which was, as Leonard Labaree has pointed out, the ideology of social immobility.[38] In this sense, it seems clear that eighteenth-century liberalism was one of the intellectual functions of groups and individuals participating in the liberalizing changes in eighteenth-century Anglo-American society.

On the whole, one might properly risk the generalization that the mind of Anglo-American society in the eighteenth century was a liberal mind—that is, more liberal than otherwise. Liberalism appears to have been, for that time, in tune with the wave of the future. The liberal ideology rested upon a basic faith in human reason, although it would be easy to overlook the fact that even the liberals recognized human nature as sometimes mean, generally self-seeking, often vicious, and prone to error:

> Reason we hear and cooly may approve;
> But all's inactive till the passions move.
> Such is the human Soul, so weak, so frail;
> Reason's her chart; but Passion is the Gale.[39]

Eighteenth-century liberalism may be identified with eighteenth-century rationalism. Liberty, in that context, was a natural condition, which had to be preserved. But what is natural is also universal: the natural rights of Americans are the natural rights of all men everywhere. Yet freedom was no mere negative condition; it was a positive force, a mechanism for the achievement of progress. This attitude, amounting in effect to a positive

[38] *Ibid.*, p. 168, *et passim.*
[39] *New York Mercury*, Jan. 8, 1759.

philosophy of liberty, was, perhaps, the true index to the eighteenth-century Anglo-American mind. Listen to Jonathan Mayhew:

> Let us all stand fast in the liberty wherewith Christ has made us free, and not suffer ourselves to be entangled with any yoke of bondage.... Let us despise the frowns and censures of those vain conceited men who set themselves up for the oracles of truth and the standard of Orthodoxy; and then call their neighbors hard names. We have not only a right to think for ourselves in matters of religion, but to act for ourselves also....
> Did I say, we have a right to judge and act for ourselves? I now add—it is our indispensable duty to do it. This is a right which we cannot relinquish, or neglect to exercise, [even] if we would, without being highly culpable; for it is absolutely unalienable in its own nature.[40]

In these samples, I think, we see evidence of a genuine liberalism. Here, by the same token, is what eighteenth-century writers might have called a pretty problem in the history of ideas.

[40] Jonathan Mayhew, *Two Objections*, pp. 8-9.

BENJAMIN FRANKLIN
AND AMERICAN LIBERALISM

IT HAS BEEN said that History has its modes; that the fashion in History-writing follows the pattern of the intellectual climate of opinion that pervades society at a given time and place. Thus the Enlightenment was characterized by the rationalistic history-writers, the early nineteenth century by the romantic historians, the late nineteenth century by the nationalists. The historians of the twentieth century, at least in the United States, are being powerfully influenced by the moods and the methods of the behavioral sciences, sociology and psychology, that is to say, in a general way in the current of historical thought represented by Karl Mannheim.

For the sociological historian, the unit-phenomenon that is the subject of his investigation is the whole society, not the individual; to him the individual is a grain of sand in a pile or a drop of water in a river; his study is concerned with the pile or the river, not the grain or the drop.

The extremists among the psychologists and the sociologists, in this school of thought, even go so far as to maintain that the individual is, in fact, merely the product of his society; his mind is formed by the social mind; his actions are entirely conditioned

[48]

by the influences exercised upon him by the society or the group in which he moves and has his being.

The historical fact that the individual is conditioned and limited by the *milieu* in which he is born and reared is, of course, obvious; it is a truism among historians today that complete historical objectivity is inconceivable, since the very thought-processes of the historian himself are profoundly conditioned by his intellectual *milieu*. At the same time, although we have long been in the habit of writing the history of social groups as units, as in the case of the city-state of Athens, or of Meiji Japan, or of the British Commonwealth of nations, we have recently been coming to recognize that the group, such as the nation, for example, may be bound together by psychological forces that make it very much more than a mere aggregation of individuals brought together only by the objectives of some common purpose. We are also coming to recognize that the nexus of psychological and intellectual ties that bind the individual in the group constitutes an historical phenomenon of major significance. It may be pertinent to inquire, nevertheless, whether this heavy emphasis upon the collective forces in human history may not unduly underrate the significance of the individual and his individual genius as a determinant in the history of a society that is of equal reality and significance with that of the collective, or social force.

The thoughts on Benjamin Franklin presented here are offered as a sort of case-study undertaken somewhat in the mood of this sociological approach to history. They are inspired by the first five volumes of the new Yale edition of Franklin's papers that have thus far appeared;[1] as those volumes cover only the years between 1720 and 1755, this essay pertains only to that period of Franklin's life.

[1] Benjamin Franklin, *The Papers of Benjamin Franklin.* Edited by Leonard Labaree and Whitfield J. Bell, Jr., 7 vols., to date (New Haven: Yale University Press, 1959——).

Max Savelle

II

Now Franklin's society, the society of Anglo-America in the four decades above indicated, was a liberal society; and Franklin, its most outstanding spokesman, was one of the greatest liberals the eighteenth century produced, either in Europe or America.

It must be recognized, of course, that it is intellectually risky to use such labels as "liberal" or "conservative" for whole societies, and it becomes necessary, right at the beginning, to explain these terms. But if a whole society may be taken as the unit-phenomenon of historical study, then it should be possible to speak accurately in terms of its "dominant" and its "recessive" characteristics—to borrow terms from the biologists.

Liberalism, as explained by Guido Ruggiero, its great historian, in the words of his English editor, R. G. Collingwood,

> begins with the recognition that men, do what we will, are free; that a man's acts are his own, spring from his own personality, and cannot be coerced.... The aim of Liberalism is to assist the individual to discipline himself and achieve his own moral progress; renouncing the two opposite errors of forcing upon him a development for which he is inwardly unprepared, and leaving him alone, depriving him of that aid to progress which a political system, wisely designed and wisely administered, can give.[2]

But Ruggiero was speaking of political liberalism. As used in this paper, the term covers this same basic position wherever observed, but it is applied to the consideration of the society's economic and social outlook, religion, education, or some other area, as well as in politics. That is to say, it was the faith of the liberals that man is by nature and by natural right free in all his activities, limited only by the lines at which his own activities impinged upon those of others.

The ideal liberal, therefore, would be one who is liberal in his

[2] Guido de Ruggiero, *The History of European Liberalism*. Translated by R. G. Collingwood (London: Oxford University Press, 1927), p. vii.

thinking with regard to all the facets of human life. Not all "liberals" are, or were, in Franklin's time; many men are—and were—liberal in certain areas of their thought, and conservative in others. By the same token, the liberal society is one in which most thoughtful individuals share the liberal outlook, in most things. It is one in which the liberal mood—as a set of ideas and habits relative to the problem of how the society is to find the good life—is the *"dominant"* mood in that society. In such a society the conservative mood, although present, might be called a *"recessive"* intellectual characteristic of the society. This does not necessarily mean that one or the other of these moods is shared by a majority of the members of the society, although the modern sociologist, with his statistical, quantitative method, might insist that, if either term means anything at all, it must mean that the mood is shared by a statistical majority of the people. The liberal mood, which I call the dominant mood of eighteenth-century Anglo-America, may, indeed have been shared by a numerical majority, although we have no way of knowing precisely. As used here, these terms mean only that one or the other of the two moods is more powerful in its influence and more characteristic of the intellectual life and the behavior of the society as a whole group than the other. Thus, when we speak of American colonial society as a liberal society it does not mean that there was not present a very considerable and powerful conservative element in it. On the contrary, there were many powerful conservative forces at work in that society; the history of liberalism in America and its eventual but temporary triumph in the generation of the Revolution is a history of its struggle against these forces, as in fact we shall see.[3]

By the same line of reasoning it may be said that France, in those four decades of the eighteenth century, was a conservative

[3] For a discussion of conservatism in colonial America, see Leonard W. Labaree, *Conservatism in Early American History* (Ithaca: Cornell University Press, Great Seal Books, 1959).

society, using the word conservative to mean devoted to the preservation of old values and old institutions against disruptive or degenerate change. There were a few liberals to be sure, such men as Diderot, Voltaire, Rousseau; but the liberal mood was as yet a "recessive" mood in French society, shared by only a very small minority of its intellectual leaders.

It is in the light of these explanations that the society of Anglo-America in the third, fourth, fifth, and sixth decades of the eighteenth century may be said to have been a liberal society. In the large, it was a society on the make, a new and rapidly expanding society in a new land, building itself along the new lines induced by the circumstances of the new land and the new experiences in it. In that society a premium was placed upon new ideas and new ways of doing things; men must be left free to think and experiment along new lines; Anglo-America was an ideal laboratory for the demonstration of the Enlightenment's faith that men are creatures endowed with intelligence, or reason, and that they can solve their problems and promote human progress indefinitely if this human reason be left free to do so.

This was the mood of the liberalism of eighteenth-century Anglo-America. In this sense, English colonial society was a liberal society. Its basic mood was expressed by Franklin's oft-quoted "Proposal for Promoting Useful Knowledge among the British Plantations in America," written in 1743,[4] which led to the organization of the American Philosophical Society in 1744:

The first Drudgery of Settling new Colonies, which confines the Attention of People to mere Necessaries, is now pretty well over; and there are many in every Province in Circumstances that set them at Ease and afford Leisure to cultivate the finer Arts, and improve the common Stock of Knowledge. To such of these who are Men of Speculation, many Hints must from time to time arise, many Observations occur, which if well-examined, pursued, and improved, might produce Discoveries to the Advantage of some or

4 Labaree, ed., *Papers of Benjamin Franklin*, II, 380-383.

all of the British plantation, or to the Benefit of Mankind in general.[5]

If we follow the modern sociologist, it seems probable that a liberal society might "condition" its members to strive for self-improvement, for change of status, by placing premiums upon innovation, invention, new ideas, education, and individual initiative. On the other hand, in a conservative society, in which status tends to be fixed and where the conservative mind thinks to preserve the status quo in all things, such phenomena are discouraged; if one is so much of an innovator as to appear to be dangerous to the status quo he is liable to the social and political sanctions of a society which disapproves of him.

It remains only to suggest that if a society conditions its individual members, so also do its individual members, each with his own peculiar genius, condition the society. It seems so obvious that Franklin was a liberal product of a liberal society that the point need not be labored; that the liberal American society was in striking measure formed by the liberal Franklin seems equally obvious.

III

Franklin was a practicing liberal in every aspect of his life during the period under discussion. For the purposes of this essay, three areas of his thought and activity have been selected for examination, in which the liberal interrelationships between him and his society seem crystal clear. The first of these is in the field of social and individual attitudes toward religion.

The most striking characteristic of religious life in pre-revolutionary Anglo-America was its heterogeneity, which derived from the fact that most of the denominations and sects of western Christendom were represented there. To which must also be added the high degree of *de facto* religious toleration that existed.

[5] *Ibid.*, II, 380.

It had not always been so. In the seventeenth century both the southern Anglicans (with the partial exception of Maryland) and the northern Calvinists (with the notable exception of Rhode Island) were practicing uniformitarians; and they had little patience with such ultra-modern, subversive ideas of religious toleration as those typified by Roger Williams. It was only in the last half of the century that a sort of toleration derived from expediency and business interest came to be advertised by the colonial proprietors and that the noble principles of William Penn began to make religious heterodoxy and mutual toleration among sects accepted realities.

But with the influx of non-English immigrants in the eighteenth century the number of new sects was multiplied. English Quakers came in considerable numbers, as did German Mennonites and Moravians, Scottish Presbyterians, English Baptists, French Huguenots, and other Christian sects, and some Jews. By the middle of the century religious heterogeneity was well-nigh universal, and religious toleration, despite the uniformitarian laws still on the statute books, was well-nigh universally accepted, both in practice and in principle. So that Franklin could demonstrate, in 1772, that the colonies were far more tolerant than the mother country.[6]

But the interests of expediency alone did not wholly explain this *de facto* toleration. Religion itself was changing in the course of the totality of American experience. Even the old doctrinal positions were changing, whether in the direction of low church democratization and dilution of the Thirty-nine Articles among the southern Anglicans, or in the rationalistic Arminianism then flourishing among the Congregationalist churches of New England, or in the reactionary neo-Calvinism of Jonathan Edwards, or in the "new light" emotionalism of the converts of the Great Awakening. Multiplicity was multiplied by multiplicity; but this was because religious ideas were changing.

[6] Benjamin Franklin, *Works* (Sparks, ed.), II, 116–117.

Everywhere the doctrinal rigidities of the seventeenth century were breaking down before the onslaughts of rationalism and a newly conceived individualism; the over-all result was a liberalization of religious doctrine. The one notable exception was Jonathan Edwards' essentially reactionary and authoritarian neo-Calvinism, the tragic failure of which lay in its inundation by the flood of liberal doctrines moving in the religious life of all the colonies. The theory of religious liberty, the hallmark of religious liberalism, was apparently a natural—perhaps an inevitable—concomitant of this liberal religious revolution.

It was in the midst of this religious revolution that Benjamin Franklin worked out his own religious outlook. Reared in a Puritan household, he rebelled against strict Puritanism and, in notable measure, but not entirely, freed himself from the conditioning that that experience represented. More broadly conditioned, it may be, by the broader intellectual and practical factors in the religious experience of his society, he passed through a series of religious positions to arrive, finally, at the simple deistic creed expressed toward the end of his life.

In the period we are discussing, as throughout his life, Franklin was a champion of freedom of religious thought and expression. In 1735, for example, he became involved in a dispute among the Presbyterians which took place over the preaching of the Reverend Mr. Samuel Hemphill. This popular preacher, whom Franklin liked, was accused of preaching unorthodox doctrines, and was censured and suspended by the Synod of Philadelphia. Franklin used the pages of the *Pennsylvania Gazette* for the publication of a vigorous defense of Hemphill's right to dissent from rigid Presbyterian orthodoxy; he also published several pamphlets and other writings dealing with the case and elaborating upon the desirability and the validity of complete religious liberty.[7]

In his famous letter of April 13, 1738, he wrote to his parents:

[7] Labaree, ed., *Papers of Benjamin Franklin*, II, 27-33; 37-88; 89-126.

Doubtless I have my Share [of erroneous opinions], and when the natural Weakness and Imperfection of Human Understanding is considered, with the unavoidable Influence of Education, Custom, Books and Company, upon our Ways of Thinking, I imagine a Man must have a good deal of Vanity who believes, and a good deal of Boldness who affirms, that all the Doctrines he holds are true; and all he rejects, are false. And perhaps the same may be justly said of every Sect, Church and Society of men when they assume to themselves that Infallibility which they deny to the Popes and Councils. I think Opinions should be judg'd of by their Influences and Effects; and if a Man holds none that tend to make him less virtuous or more vicious, it may be concluded he holds none that are dangerous; which I hope is the case with me.... But since it is no more in a Man's Power to think than to look like another, methinks all that should be expected from me is to keep my Mind open to Conviction, to hear patiently and examine attentively whatever is offered me for that end; ....[8]

It may be *ex post facto* reasoning, but it certainly appears that Franklin had learned—had been "conditioned," to use the modern psychologists' jargon—by his experience in the Hemphill incident and others like it. The incident itself was one with broad social ramifications, one which was, indeed, typical of the struggles of religious liberty against the old religious order. Franklin's involvement in it was an individual involvement in a social experience: conditioned by it, he then turned his convictions as to the validity of religious freedom into a variety of channels through which he deliberately sought to lead his society toward a more liberal philosophy and practice in religious matters.

It is to be kept in mind that this single battle was lost; Hemphill was suspended and conservatives among the Presbyterian clergy had the satisfaction of silencing his dissent. It is even to be supposed that their conservative position was accepted by the rank and file of the Presbyterian congregations. Furthermore, this victory of conservatism may be taken as an incident in the broad conservative defense of orthodoxy in all the colonies.

[8] *Ibid.*, II, 202–204.

But it was a Pyrrhic victory. And the campaign of Franklin for freedom of religious dissent was echoed throughout the colonies— by those who, like the rationalist Jonathan Mayhew in Massachusetts, demanded religious and intellectual freedom for the sake of the rational discovery of truth, as well as those who, like the Presbyterian Samuel Davies in Virginia, for reasons of expediency, demanded the freedom to operate Presbyterian churches in an officially Anglican Virginia.

The winds of religious freedom were unquestionably blowing in colonial America; Franklin felt and enjoyed the winds, and added a few gusty blasts of his own.

IV

The second area of liberal interrelationships between Franklin and his society to be examined here is that of education. The first colonists had gone to America with the educational attitudes and habits they had had in England. For the first generation of Englishmen in America, as Bernard Bailyn has recently suggested,[9] education was largely informal and "instinctive"; its chief instrumentalities were the family, the church, and the community:

> Despite a considerable amount of occupational mobility [says Bailyn] the normal expectation was that the child would develop along familiar lines, that the divergence of his career from that of his parents' and grandparents' would be limited, and that he could proceed with confidence and security along a well-worn path whose turnings and inclines had long been known and could be dealt with by measures specified by tradition.[10]

In other words, the educational outlook and practice of the first generation were calculated to transmit the culture of the old generation to the new substantially without change. Education itself was an instinctive sociological process that called for little

[9] Bernard Bailyn, *Education in the Forming of American Society: Needs and Opportunities for Study* (Chapel Hill: University of North Carolina Press, 1960).

[10] *Ibid.*, p. 20.

[57]

formal thought or deliberate planning. This type of educational process, one whose objective is the transmission of a relatively fixed culture without change, is properly to be called conservative education.

By the middle of the eighteenth century American education had undergone a profound revolution. From an automatic, instinctive function of the sociological process as a whole, education had become "an instrument of deliberate social purpose";[11] the family institution had lost its central place in society, and the church had ceased to be the focal point of social purpose. Education had become deliberate, formal; its new chief mechanism was the school. Education itself was now a mechanism for the promotion of culture in a fluid society, a society in almost constant change, a society in which new divergences from old ways were likely to be at a premium.

> But education [to quote Bailyn again] not only reflects and adjusts to society, once formed, it turns back upon it and acts upon it.... Education ... had proved in itself to be an agency of rapid social change, a powerful internal accelerator.... Second, education as it emerged from the colonial period has distinctively shaped the American personality; it has contributed much to the forming of national character. [This character] emerged from the processes of education which tended to isolate the individual, to propel him away from the simple acceptance of a predetermined role, and to nourish his distrust of authority.[12]

It is in the light of this concept of the nature of education in colonial America that Benjamin Franklin is to be seen, both as a product and as a director of the education influence here described. It is true, of course, that Franklin was self-educated and that he began his education in the early mould and completed it in the new.

Franklin's liberal responses to the socio-educational revolution going on about him are to be seen in many of his activities and writings. His association with the Junto, the Library Company,

---

[11] *Ibid.*, p. 22. [12] *Ibid.*, pp. 48–49.

and the American Philosophical Society were all inspired by the moods of self-improvement, of individual economic, social and intellectual movement, and of the social values implied in the free exchange of ideas.

In his most famous piece on education, his *Proposals Relating to the Education of Youth in Pensilvania,*[13] Franklin's liberal thinking on the subject of education became explicit. Drawing extensively upon the writings of Locke, Turnbull and others, Franklin laid down a secular program of education that embodied a radical modification of older educational objectives and ideals. He concluded with an eloquent expression of his own idea as to what the aim of the liberal education ought to be:

> With the whole should be constantly inculcated and cultivated that *Benignity of Mind* which shows itself in *searching for* and *seizing* every opportunity *to serve* and *to oblige;* and is the Foundation of what is called GOOD BREEDING; being highly useful to the Possessor, and most agreeable to all.

> The idea of what is *true Merit,* should also be often presented to Youth, explain'd and impress'd on their Minds as consisting in an *Inclination* join'd with an *Ability* to serve Mankind, one's Country, Friends, and Family; which *Ability* is (with the Blessing of God) to be acquir'd or greatly encreased by *true learning;* and should indeed be the great *Aim* and *End* of all Learning.[14]

For Franklin, the school should be an agency for the deliberate conditioning of men for the free exercise of their intellects and for the conscious moulding of society. It represented an institution to prepare men to live in what Bailyn calls "an open-ended universe"; that is, a society in which they must be, above all things, adaptable, prepared for "such a tour of surprises as he [Franklin] had known." "Thus instructed," said Franklin in his *Idea of the English School,* "youth will come out of this school fitted for learning any business, calling or profession."[15]

13 Philadelphia, 1749. Reprinted in Labaree, ed., *Papers of Benjamin Franklin,* III, 395–421.
14 *Ibid.,* III, 418–419.
15 *Ibid.,* III, 108.

Franklin had taught himself, in the midst of a changing society, to be an adaptable, self-directing, and cultivated human being, always prepared to accept, and to benefit from, the new changes that he was likely to meet almost daily. He had exploited to the utmost the values of his sort of education in his own experience. He proposed to make the same sort of education available to his fellow-citizens by the establishment of a school whose curriculum would institutionalize the educational values suitable to a society characterized by fluidity and change. His proposals were realized in practice by the establishment of the Philadelphia academy; through it, his personal influence was observably exercised in the formation of the educational theory and practice of American society.

V

In the third area of Franklin's intellectual life the interrelationship between his ideas and the liberalism of his society is particularly clear. This was the area of the freedom of the press.

In this area, again, there is to be noted a transition from a predominantly conservative mood in society in the seventeenth century to a mood that by 1750 was moving strongly in the direction of a liberal attitude toward the press and its social function.[16]

There was, in fact, very little printing of any kind in Anglo-America in the seventeenth century. The first press had been inaugurated at Cambridge, Massachusetts, in 1638, and this press alone, among the printing ventures of the century, as a sort of official publishing house, enjoyed an active and relatively distinguished career. But this press was the exception, not the rule. The prevailing mood, in all the colonies, was distinctly opposed to the existence of a free press. About 1670 Governor William

---

[16] For a brilliant discussion of the culmination of this process in the decade prior to the American Revolution, see Arthur M. Schlesinger, *Crisis in Freedom* (Cambridge: Harvard University Press, 1958).

Franklin and American Liberalism

Berkeley thanked his God that there were no printing presses to stir up the people in Virginia; in 1662 the colony of Massachusetts had enacted a law requiring that the manuscript of every proposed publication be submitted to the official board of censors for approval before printing. Under this regime publication of *The Imitation of Christ* was held up until certain papistical passages were excised.[17] Colonial governors were regularly instructed "to provide that noe person have any press for printing, nor that any book, or other matters whatsoever be printed without ... especial leave to license first obtained."[18]

William Nuthead opened a press at Jamestown in Virginia in 1682, only to have it suppressed a few months later by royal order for publishing certain documents without prior permission. William Bradford opened a press in Philadelphia in 1685 but presently moved to New York in search of a more congenial climate for his product. Richard Pierce and Benjamin Harris published one issue of their first American newspaper, *Public Occurrences,* at Boston in September of 1690, only to have it promptly suppressed by the Governor. James Franklin's *New England Courant* was suppressed and Franklin spent some time in jail because of its criticism of the Governor and Council of Massachusetts. James Franklin moved to Newport, Rhode Island, to found the *Rhode Island Gazette;* James's apprentice, younger brother Benjamin, had long since sought a more liberal *milieu* in Philadelphia.

Theoretically, at least, colonial printers were subject to the English Press Restriction Acts, the last of which expired in 1695. They were held strictly responsible to the legislatures of their colonies, and they were subject to the English laws of libel, under which the judges decided if printed matter was libelous and the juries decided only upon the fact of publication. Furthermore,

17 Hellmut Lehmann-Haupt, *The Book in America* (2d ed.; New York: R. R. Bowker Co., 1951), p. 43.
18 Quoted, *ibid.*, p. 43.

[61]

they were under almost irresistible pressure from vested-interest groups, such as the clergy. Exposed to all varieties of reactionary, authoritarian pressures, the life of the printer was not an easy one.

The practical needs of the community, nevertheless, forced upon it an acceptance of printing establishments, especially after the turn of the century. The first regular newspaper, *The Boston News-Letter,* was started in 1704, and in the half-century that followed newspapers began to be published in nearly all the colonies; in some of them, by 1760, there were several newspapers.

It was in these fifty or sixty years that the society of the thirteen continental colonies which eventually seceded from the Empire went through its liberal revolution and became, in the broad sense already defined, a liberal society. As a part of the liberal revolution, too, the press became an instrument of significant social utility and enjoyed a remarkable growth of freedom. Suppressive laws remained on the books, to be sure; censorship, official and unofficial, continued to plague the printers; and the ancient principles of libel remained almost intact, as embodied in the laws, until after the Revolution.

Yet the intellectual climate was changing. As early as 1696 a jury in Salem, Massachusetts, defied the presiding judge and declared Thomas Maule not guilty of libel for publishing facts, at the same time asserting the revolutionary doctrine that publishing the facts was not necessarily libel and that the printer had a right to publish them. The jury in the famous case of John Peter Zenger, in New York (1734), did the same thing; and Zenger's counsel, Andrew Hamilton of Pennsylvania, after a most eloquent assertion of the intellectual validity and the social utility of the liberty of the press, was given a popular ovation and the freedom of the city of New York in recognition of his "learned and generous defence of the rights of mankind, and the liberty of the press."[19]

[19] Vincent Buranelli, ed., *The Trial of Peter Zenger* (New York: New York University Press, 1957), p. 133.

Many other statements and defenses of the principles of the liberty of publication, whether in newspapers or books or elsewhere, found expression in Angloamerica in the eighteenth century; and the Continental Congress was engaging in no idle talk, in its address to the Canadians in 1774, when it pointed to freedom of the press as one of the most sacred rights of Americans and proclaimed the thirteen colonies to be the most liberal society in the world in this regard.

Meanwhile, Benjamin Franklin, down in Philadelphia, was continually voicing the increasingly liberal moods of his society in his life-long battle for publishing freedom. Already, as a boy, he had encountered the evils of suppression of the press when he saw his brother James jailed by the Massachusetts authorities for publishing remarks that were indirectly critical of them. And on that occasion, as *ad interim* editor of the *New England Courant,* Benjamin had reprinted one of *Cato's Letters* from the *London Journal,* arguing the principle of freedom of the press and lamenting the evils that inevitably sprang from censorship.[20] When he had embarked upon his own publishing enterprise in Philadelphia, Franklin repeatedly rang the changes on the principle of the freedom of printers and publishers.

Here are some sample paragraphs from his "Apology for Printers," published in the *Pennsylvania Gazette* in 1731, stated as the governing principles of printers in general,

1. That the Opinions of Men are almost as various as their Faces; an Observation general enough to become a common Proverb, *So many Men so many Minds. . . .*

5. Printers are educated in the Belief, that when Men differ in Opinion, both Sides ought equally to have the Advantage of being heard by the Publick; and that when Truth and Error have fair Play, the former is always an overmatch for the latter: Hence they chearfully serve all contending Writers that pay them well, without regarding on which side they are of the Question in Dispute. . . .

20 Labaree, ed., *The Papers of Benjamin Franklin,* I, 27ff.

8. That if all Printers were determin'd not to print any thing till they were sure it would offend no body, there would be very little printed.[21]

Franklin published in the *Gazette* a sympathetic account of the Zenger trial, and on November 17, 1737, he printed a long essay "On Freedom of Speech and the Press" (which was formerly attributed to Franklin but which has been shown by his present editors to have been by another hand).[22] He returned to the theme in 1740 with a "Statement of Editorial Policy" in the *Pennsylvania Gazette* of July 24, 1740. Here he says that

> It is a Principle among Printers, that when Truth has fair Play, it will always prevail over Falsehood; therefore, though they have an undoubted Property in their own Press, yet they willingly allow, that anyone is entitled to the Use of it, who thinks it necessary to offer his Sentiments on disputable Points to the Publick, and will be at the Expense of it. If what is thus publish'd be good, Mankind has the Benefit of it: If it be bad...[,] the more 'tis made publick, the more its Weakness is exposed, and the greater Disgrace falls upon the Author, whoever he be: who is at the same Time depriv'd of an Advantage he would otherwise without fail make use of, viz., of Complaining, that Truth is suppressed; and *that he could say* MIGHTY MATTERS, *had he but the Opportunity of being heard*....[23]

It is difficult to avoid the conclusion that Franklin's devotion to the principles of freedom of the press was a response both to the experience he had as an apprentice and to the ideas he had absorbed from an intellectual atmosphere typified by *Cato's Letters*. There must have been something in the social *milieu* in his daily contacts with his fellow men, that invited the publication of his ideas. It may have been discussions around the coffee-tables where businessmen congregated; even if Franklin's publications on the theme were born of controversy, the mere fact of the existence of controversy is evidence enough that there were men who argued the liberal principle against the con-

[21] *Ibid.*, I, 194, 195.
[22] *Ibid.*, II, 184.
[23] *Ibid.*, II, 260.

servatives who opposed it. Franklin was not a publicist who would publish material of this nature without the assurance of having an audience to read it.

The freedom of the press had become, by 1750, a matter of import to many of the liberals in American society. The Zenger case is only one dramatic illustration of the growing American concern for this freedom. The newspapers were not yet considered organs for the formation of opinion; that was to wait until the era of the Revolution. What was demanded was the freedom to publish information and secondary opinion thought to be of utility to society.

Franklin lived and moved in the midst of this mood; he was conditioned by it, and he, in turn, significantly contributed to its shaping. It is beside the point to recognize the fact that there was a lag of half a century between the widespread popular acceptance of the *idea* and the revision of the *laws* relative to the press on the statute books. What we are here interested in is a mood—a phenomenon in the history of ideas. And that mood, in Anglo-America *ca.* 1750-1760, was real.

On the basis of what seems to be the evidence, then, there is to be observed a close and clear interrelationship in the period between 1720 and 1755 between Franklin's growing liberalism and that of his society. Franklin's experiences in his society and in his intellectual *milieu* seem unquestionably to have conditioned him toward liberalism. Conversely, his influence upon his society—indeed, upon the intellectual life of the entire western world of his time—was exercised in the direction of cultivating and promoting a liberal outlook in that society.

Merely to conclude that the historian or the biographer must attempt to show a man's influence upon the mind of his society would be, of course, to conclude nothing new: historians and biographers have been doing that ever since Thucydides and Plutarch. What is new is the new dimensions given to society, to the individual, and to history by the behavioral scientific approach to human studies. Accepting (with some caution) the new dimensions suggested by the behavioralists and taking a man like Franklin as a case study, the historian must recognize on the basis of the scientific evidence, what the behavioralists call the "conditioning" of the individual by his society, and try to evaluate it. On the other hand, however, he must point out to the behavioralist that social conditioning is probably not the only factor in the formation of the individual. For the historical evidence is overwhelmingly on the side of concluding that such an individual as Franklin certainly appears historically to have been innately endowed with a peculiar individual differentness and genius that made it possible for him actually to "condition" his society.

Perhaps the scientific historian may have something to contribute to the work of the behavioral scientists.

PART II

The Colonies in America

THE APPEARANCE OF AN AMERICAN
ATTITUDE TOWARD EXTERNAL AFFAIRS,
1750-1775

In the *Pennsylvania Gazette* of January 15, 1751, appears the following jingle, which was copied from the English *Westminster Journal* of October 8, 1750:

> While Britain complains of *Neutrality* broke,
>   De Puysieux collogues like a subtle Iago,
> And tells us his King will *restore* at a stroke,
>   St. Lucia, St. Vincent, Domin'ca, Tobago.
>
> But while they *croud People*, and *fortify Bays*,
>   The Talks at *Barbados* unless they will wink-a,
> Must see the *French settling*, whate'er Puysieux says,
>   St. Vincent, St. Lucia, Tobago, Domin'ca.
>
> Shall Britons believe, when *both Parties* are heard,
>   Our *Creole* all *Sland'rers*, their *Neighbours* all inn'cent?
> Or claim, with a *Lye*, giv'n to each *Frenchman's Beard*,
>   Domin'ca, Tobago, St. Lucia, St. Vincent?
>
> To settle this Point send out *forty good Sail*,
>   With Warren or Hawke to inspect each *Minutia;*
> They'll teach us *to whom shall belong*, without fail,
>   Tobago, Domin'ca, St. Vincent, St. Lucia.[1]

This political doggerel refers to the dispute then going on between France and England over the so-called "neutral Islands"

[1] *Pennsylvania Gazette*, Jan. 15, 1751.

of the West Indies. The fact that the verses were copied in an American newspaper is fairly revealing; for it throws light upon an American interest in international affairs that was both wide and deep.

It is a significant fact that American colonial newspapers contain a much greater proportion of foreign news than do the newspapers of the nineteenth century. This is a clear indication that Americans, in the period before the Revolution, were much more actively and intensely concerned with the affairs of the outside world than they were after the end of the Napoleonic Wars and after President Monroe had slammed the door in Europe's face in 1823.

Certainly as long as the French and their Indian allies, both great and terrible enemies, stood athwart the westward march to empire, the British-Americans were bound to watch closely every move of the great European imperial rivals. This had to be, since the very survival of the British colonies might well depend upon the fickle behavior of the scales in the European balance of power. Moreover, there were weightier reasons for an interest in European international affairs close at hand. Frenchmen had been fighting Englishmen for the wilderness ever since the beginnings of English and French colonization; and that conflict had its roots and its reasons for being here in America and would probably have had to be fought out even had France and England never raised a hand against each other. But they had, and the local American conflict was part of the larger imperial competition around the world. The Americans knew it; and they also knew that their own fate might well hang upon the outcome of this first world war. Their interest in the Anglo-French conflict, therefore, sprang from involvements in it that were vital to them.

But the Americans were not deeply interested in this struggle of the titans merely because they were tied to one of them. The fact that they were the offspring of England gave them a psychological and emotional tie of loyalty that probably would have kept alive in them an interest in England and all things English, even had there been no Anglo-French conflict. Yet the two things went together; the need for protection combined with patriotic attachment in the mid-eighteenth century to produce a burst of British-American patriotism that has seldom, if ever, been equaled.

The colonial newspapers of the 1750's were full of it; it found expression both in patriotic and anti-French news and articles copied from English newspapers and in diatribes composed by Americans.[2] At the same time, the official attitude, represented by such men as Governors James Glen of South Carolina, Robert Dinwiddie of Virginia, Horatio Sharpe of Maryland, and William Shirley of Massachusetts, was one of patriotic alarm. This alarm was expressed by Governor Sharpe of Maryland, for example, who saw the French occupation of the upper Allegheny Valley as early as March 6, 1754, as "flagrant Acts of Hostility ... an Invasion ... [and] unjust Usurpations and Encroachments on his Majesty's Dominions."[3] To which the Maryland assembly coolly made reply that

> ... we humbly conceive, that the Situation ... of our Neighbours of Virginia, with regard to any Violence or Outrage, threatened or perpetrated against them, by the French, does not require our immediate aid or Assistance, by the raising of an armed Force here ... and therefore, we do not think it necessary to do any Thing in that Matter at present.[4]

Needless to say, the official alarm of the governors was shared by the imperialists in all the colonies, but particularly in those which had frontiers in the areas claimed by both French and English. Such imperialists, for example, were Dr. William Clarke

[2] See, for example, the *Maryland Gazette*, Aug. 15, 1750; *ibid.*, Sept. 6, 1749; *Pennsylvania Gazette, passim; South-Carolina Gazette,* July 23, 1750, *et passim;* etc.

[3] *Maryland Archives,* L, 422–23.

[4] *Ibid.,* L, 428.

of Boston[5] and William Livingston of New York. Clarke evaded the question of just boundaries between the French colonies and the British, and claimed that the French had "a plan" which, if successfully carried out, could result only in the domination of the British-American colonies by France. The British colonies, he said, were doubling in population every twenty years, and would in the future consume enormous quantities of British manufactures; but he warned that this great market and source of material strength would be lost to Britain if France were allowed to seize the British colonies. In fact, he said, "the Prince, who holds Possession of the *English* Colonies in *North-America,* will be in a Condition to keep the Sovereignty of the Atlantic Ocean, thro' which the homeward bound Trade from the East and West-Indies generally passes."[6] In short, if France takes the British colonies, he wrote, British commerce will be destroyed; and, with it, Britain.

This thoroughly mercantilistic argument was echoed by William Livingston, who elaborated it into an American version of the theory of the balance of power as dependent upon colonial commerce. For Livingston saw the colonies as an inexhaustible magazine of national wealth, "and if suffered to fall into the hands of the French, such will be the accession to their [France's] already extended commerce and marine strength, that Great Britain must not only lose her former lustre, but, dreadful even in thought! cease to be any longer an independent power." Nay, he says, it would bring to pass "the long-projected design of that aspiring nation, for setting up an Universal Monarchy: for, if France rule the ocean, her resources will enable her to subject all Europe to her sway."[7]

The attitude of many American officials and imperialists was

[5] William Clarke, *Observations on the Late and Present Conduct of the French . . . in North America* (Boston, 1755).

[6] Clarke, p. 43.

[7] William Livingston, *A Review of the Military Operations in North America . . .* (Dublin, 1757), p. 3.

thus distinctly mercantilist in nature. Needless to say, these imperialists were none too scrupulous about the validity of their claims to the lands beyond the Allegheny watershed, and they were all for the "offensive defensive" to beat the French to them.[8]

There were some American imperialists, on the other hand,

---

[8] The word "mercantilist" is used here to indicate the political philosophy that dominated the minds of most European statesmen in the middle of the eighteenth century. This was a body of ideas that varied from statesman to statesman and from country to country, but it held, in general, that the power of a state rests ultimately upon the extent and the profitableness of its commerce. Colonies, in such a polity, were regarded as being areas of the national market, to be monopolized, as far as possible, by the mother country; as sources of raw materials to be exploited as exclusively as possible by the mother country; and as having a commerce of their own that was to be encouraged only so long as it redounded, in the long run, to the profit of the mother country and to be discouraged in every point where it seemed to be in rivalry with the commerce of the mother country or where it appeared to cause a net loss to the merchants of the mother country. For example, as Professor C. W. Alvord has shown in his *Mississippi Valley in British Politics* (2 vols., Cleveland, 1917), the British mercantilists were divided over the policy Britain should follow with regard to the Mississippi Valley, because they could not agree whether settlement of the valley or reservation of the area for the fur trade with the Indians would be more profitable for British commerce as a whole. Mercantilism was the sort of thinking that led General Thomas Gage to oppose settlement of the valley because he thought the colonists there would not send their products to the English market: "I [think it would] be for our interest to keep the Settlers within reach of the Sea-Coast as long as we can; and to cramp their Trade as far as it can be done prudently. Cities flourish and increase by extensive Trade, artisans and Mechanicks of all Sort's are drawn thither, who teach all sorts of handicraft work before unknown in the Country, and they soon come to make for themselves what they used to import. I have seen this Increase, and I assure your Lordship that Foundations are laid in Philadelphia that must create Jealousy in an Englishman." Thomas Gage, *The Correspondence of General Thomas Gage*, ed. by Clarence E. Carter (2 vols., New Haven, 1933), II, 616.

In the realm of international relations it was this same mercantilist philosophy which led the duc de Choiseul to write, in 1758, that "The King [of France] believes, Monsieur, that it is possessions in America that will in the future form the balance of power in Europe, and that, if the English invade that [the Spanish] part of the world, as it appears they have the intention of doing, it will result therefrom that England will usurp the commerce of the nations, and that she alone will remain rich in Europe." AE. Cor. Pol. Naples, 78: 44–54; quoted in Max Savelle, "The American Balance of Power and European Diplomacy," in R. B. Morris, ed., *The Era of the American Revolution* (New York, 1939), pp. 160–61.

[73]

who, like Thomas Lee of Virginia, were more interested in land than they were in commerce. Lee, as is well known, was the moving spirit in the Ohio Company, and extremely active in trying to arouse support in other colonies for his belief that Britain owned America all the way to the Pacific and his own frank purpose "to extend the British empire"[9] by defeating the French on the Ohio.

The alarm and the aggressiveness of the imperialists were not shared by the colonial assemblies, however. Several of the assemblies, if not all, were distinctly cool, to say the least, toward the official and journalistic patriotic fervor. The Maryland assembly refused to grant any money to aid Virginia until after Washington's defeat at Fort Necessity, and the Pennsylvania assembly, even as late as January, 1755, remarked to their governor that the French activities in the west seemed to have been exaggerated; the territory involved, they said, lay in Virginia anyway: why should Pennsylvania concern itself?[10] The New York assembly, which might have been expected to be interested in westward expansion, stated flatly that the building of a fort by the French at French Creek "may, but does not by any Evidence or Information, appear to us to be an Invasion, of any of his Majesty's Colonies, nor does the Government of *Virginia,* seem to look upon it as such," since Dinwiddie's letter appealing for aid says only that "the Plan of Operation is no more, than to take Possession of the Lands in his Majesty's Name, and build Forts agree-

---

[9] Quoted in Kenneth P. Bailey, *The Ohio Company of Virginia* (Glendale, 1939), p. 39. See also *Minutes of the Provincial Council of Pennsylvania,* V, 422, *et passim.* It should be remembered that the Anglo-French competition in North America was part of a world-wide conflict of mercantilist empires, and that the rival penetrations of the Ohio Valley were only one scene in the North American theater which must be studied along with the concurrent disputes over Acadia and the Neutral Islands. Title to the upper Ohio was certainly not clear, either to the French or to the British, although the French seem to have had a little the best of the argument. In Acadia, on the other hand, the positions were reversed, and the British claims were probably more justified than the French.

[10] *Pennsylvania Gazette,* Jan. 7, 1755.

able to his Command."[11] Even the Virginia House of Burgesses, of all the colonial assemblies the one most directly interested in the French movements, attached to the bill appropriating £20,-000 for the support of measures to be taken to defend the Virginia frontier a rider requiring that £2,500 be paid to Peyton Randolph as agent representing the house of burgesses in London![12] This action was bitterly protested by Dinwiddie, rejected by the council as "an Alteration of the Constitution," and defended by the burgesses as "agreeable to the Usage of Parliament." Furthermore, they said, although for patriotic reasons they would not insist upon the point, they felt sure that their conduct would be "such an undeniable Testimony to Posterity of our strict Attachment to their [*i.e.*, posterity's] Rights and Properties, that should they ever be so unhappy as to groan under the galling Yoke of civil and religious Oppression, it could not be the Effect of any Inactivity, Supineness, or Neglect in us, the faithful Guardians of their Liberties."[13]

Aside from the religious scruples of the Quakers in Pennsylvania, it seems evident that the coolness of the colonial assemblies toward the Anglo-French conflict, marked by their reactions both to Dinwiddie's appeals and to the Albany Plan of Union in 1754, is to be explained largely in terms of their struggle for political autonomy and against prerogative, whether royal or proprietary.

When we observe the popular reactions to the Anglo-French conflict, however, it becomes crystal clear that most articulate Americans were ardent British patriots. Dr. William Douglass of Boston probably expressed the thought of many of his fellow citizens when he wrote, late in the 1740's, that

The French are the common Nusance and Disturbers of Europe, and will in a short time become the same in *America,* if not mu-

---

[11] *Journal of the Votes and Proceedings of the General Assembly of the Colony of New York* (2 vols., New York, 1766), II, 378–79.
[12] *Journals of the House of Burgesses of Virginia, 1752–1755; 1756–1758,* ed. by H. R. McIlwaine (Richmond, 1919), p. 201.
[13] *Ibid.,* p. 211.

tilated at Home, and in *America* fenced off from us by Ditches and
Walls, that is, by great Rivers and impracticable Mountains....
*By Custom Time out of Mind, they are above, and do upon all
Occasions dispense with the Principles of Honesty and Honour;*
Superiority and Power is their only Rule, as Louis XIV modestly
expressed it, in the Device upon his Cannon, *Ratio ultima Regum:*
They occasionally make *Dupes* of the other Princes in Europe;
their Promises and Faith are by them used only as a sort of Scaf-
folding, which, when the Structure is finished, or Project effected,
they drop; in all publick Treaties they are *Gens de mauvaise
Foy....* [They are] more capable of swarming into their Colonies
than we are; in order to preserve a Ballance in *Europe,* they ought
to be curtail'd or dismembered there, which will effectually at the
same Time prevent their too great Growth in America.[14]

The hatred of France and all things French was complemented
by love of Britain, and celebrated in patriotic speeches that have
a familiar ring, even today. Consider, for example, the election
sermon of the Reverend Jonathan Mayhew, in 1754, in which the
preacher exhorts his countrymen to protect the free, British-
American way of life against the unspeakable danger of domination by French autocracy:

And what horrid scene is this, which restless, roving fancy, or
something of an higher nature, presents to me, and so chills my
blood! Do I behold these territories of freedom, become the prey of
arbitrary power?...Do I see the slaves of Lewis with their Indian
allies, dispossessing the free-born [American] subjects of King
George, of the inheritance received from their forefathers, and
purchased by them at the expense of their ease, their treasure, their
blood!...Do I see a protestant, there, stealing a look at his bible,
and being tak[en] in the fact, punished like a felon!...Do I see all
liberty, property, religion, happiness, changed, or rather trans-
substantiated, into slavery, poverty, superstition, wretchedness![15]

Or this, by the Reverend Samuel Davies, of Virginia:

And shall these Ravages go on uncheck'd? Shall *Virginia* incur
the Guilt, and the everlasting Shame of tamely exchanging her

[14] William Douglass, *A Summary, Historical and Political, of the British
Settlements on North America* (Boston, 1749–52), I, 2–3.
[15] Jonathan Mayhew, *Election Sermon, 1754,* pp. 37–38, quoted in Alice M.
Baldwin, *The New England Clergy and the American Revolution* (Durham,
N. C., 1928), p. 87.

Liberty, her Religion, and her All, for arbitrary *Gallic* Power, and for Papish Slavery, Tyranny, and Massacre? Alas! are there none of her Children, that enjoyed all the Blessings of her Peace, that will espouse her Cause, and befriend her now in the Time of her Danger? Are *Britons* utterly degenerated by so short a Remove from their Mother-Country? Is the Spirit of Patriotism entirely extinguished among us? And must I give thee up for lost, O my Country! and all that is included in that important word?[16]

The patriotism to which these men appealed was very real. Nor was it confined to politicians and preachers, for it permeated every form of expression. As might be expected, it is often to be encountered in the budding native poetry. For example, John Maylem of Newport prayed for power to avenge the monstrous perfidy of the French in his poem "Gallic Perfidy":

> Amazing Perfidy! . . .
>   Ye Powers of Fury lend
> Some mighty Phrensy to enrage my Brest
> With solemn Song, beyond all Nature's Strain! . . .
> O Chief in War! of all (young) Albion's Force,
> Invest me only with sufficient Power;
> I (yet a Boy) will play the Man, and chase
> The wily Savage from his secret Haunts:
> Not Alpine Mounts shall thwart my rapid Course;
> I'll scale the Craggs, then, with impetuous Speed,
> Rush down the Steep, and scow'r along the Vale;
> Then on the Sea-Shore halt; and last, explore
> The green Meanders of eternal Wood.[17]

And young Francis Hopkinson, budding poet of the Philadelphia salon, celebrated the fall of Louisbourg in 1758 in lines that are both patriotic and aristocratic:

> At length 'tis done! The glorious conflict's done!
> And *British* valour has the conquest won!
> *Success* our arms, our heroes, *Honor* crowns,
> And Louisbourg an *English* monarch owns. . . . .

---

[16] Samuel Davies, *Religion and Patriotism the Constituents of a Good Soldier* (Philadelphia, 1756), pp. 4–5.

[17] Quoted in Lawrence C. Wroth, "John Maylem: Poet and Warrior," *Publications of the Colonial Society of Massachusetts*, XXXIX, 87–120, pp. 100–101.

Give your loose canvas to the breezes free
Ye floating thund'rers, bulwarks of the sea!
Haste bear the joyful tidings to your king,
And with the voice of war declare 'tis Victory you bring.
Let the wild *Croud* that catch the breath of fame,
In mad *Huzzas* their ruder joys proclaim;
Let their loud thanks to Heav'n in flames ascend,
Whilst mingling shouts the azure concave rend.
But let the *Few,* whom *Reason* makes more wise,
In tears of *Gratitude* uplift their eyes;
Oh may their breasts dilate with *sober* joy,
Let Pray'r their hearts, their tongues let *Praise* employ!
To bless our *God* with me let all unite;
He guides the conqu'ring sword, *he* governs in the fight.[18]

"If ever there was a national war," wrote Benjamin Franklin in 1760, "this [the Seven Years' War] is truly such a one; a war in which the interest of the whole [Anglo-American] nation is directly and fundamentally concerned."[19]

These were British-American patriots; and they meant what they said. Furthermore, they did not think of themselves as separate from the British Empire but as integral parts of it. They and their immediate interests were intimately concerned in the Anglo-French conflict; their official connection with Britain as an organic part of the empire made an interest in the world relationships of their empire seem only natural; and self-interest and imperial outlook were bolstered by a very real British-American patriotism.

The wave of British-American patriotism that swept through the colonies between 1754 and 1760 probably may have expressed the feelings of the majority of the Americans. At the same time, even in the midst of war, the colonial assemblies continued to be jealous of their rights and privileges, and to eye with a certain amount of distrust the moves of the British government and of

[18] Francis Hopkinson, "Poem on the Taking of Cap Breton," *American Magazine*, I, no. 11 (August, 1758), 551–54.

[19] Benjamin Franklin, *The Works of Benjamin Franklin*, ed. by Jared Sparks (10 vols., Boston, 1840), IV, 21.

the British commanders in America. As soon as the war was over, American distrust of British motives, coupled with the colonial dislike of the patronizing airs of their English cousins, broke out into the open, and the Americans began to ask, "Who won the war, anyway?" This remarkable attitude, implying the conviction that the American colonies were of great importance in the empire and to the world at large, was not without precedent, for there were a good many Americans like William Clarke who felt that it was the New England expedition against Cape Breton in 1745, that had "compelled Louisbourg to surrender and gave Peace to Europe."[20] And there were a good many, including Clarke and Livingston, who were coming to the conviction that the real makeweight in the international balance of power, after all, was America, and that the chief source of Britain's predominant strength in the balance of forces in Europe was precisely her American colonies.

These are evidences of the growing sense of self-realization among the Americans. And this growing self-assurance was unquestionably one of the psychological factors that emboldened the Americans to resist the Grenville program of reorganization after the Seven Years' War was over. As the American resistance grew, and the debate waxed warm, Daniel Dulany brought the "who-won-the-war" question right out into the open and stated it in the following explicit terms:

> It is presumed that it was a notable service done by *New England,* when the militia of that colony reduced *Cape-Breton,* since it enabled the *British ministers* to make a peace less disadvantageous and inglorious than they otherwise must have been constrained to submit to, in the humble state to which they were then reduced.... [Furthermore, it is clear] that the general exertion of *the colonies in North America,* during the last war [1756-1763], not only facilitated, but was indispensably requisite to the success of those operations by which so many glorious conquests were achieved, and that those conquests have put it in the power of the present illustrious ministers to make a peace upon terms of

20 Clarke, p. iv.

[79]

so much glory and advantage, as to afford an inexhaustible subject during their administration, and the triumph of toryism, at least, for their ingenious panegyrists to celebrate. . . .

An *American,* without justly incurring the imputation of ingratitude, may doubt, whether some other motive, besides pure generosity, did not prompt the *British Nation* to engage in the defense of the colonies. He may be induced to think that the measures taken for the protection of the plantations, were not only connected with the interests, but [were] even necessary to the defense of *Great-Britain* herself, because he may have reason to imagine that Great-Britain, could not long subsist as an independent kingdom after the loss of her colonies.[21]

This sort of thinking betrays a new mood—or rather the maturation of an old one—among the Americans. Not only were they the decisive factor in the winning of the war for Great Britain, according to Dulany; they were absolutely necessary to Britain's continued survival: and Britain had better have a care to treat them with respect.

As the debate blew hot and cold between 1765 and 1775, but generally hotter, the orientation of the Americans toward the continuing Anglo-French rivalry slowly shifted. It is true that the newspapers contained brief notices of French actions, the movements of the French fleet, and the like, and spoke of the French people as "our" enemies;[22] but such news items were relatively rare. Space was now filled up with the "Virginia Resolves," the "Massachusetts Resolves," Dickinson's *Letters of a Pennsylvania Farmer,* and other discussions of the relationships of the colonies with the empire. The interest of the Americans was now obviously directed toward American relations with Great Britain rather than with other parts of the world. As is well known, the Americans were now struggling to find a definition of their place in the British Empire that would be conformable both to their ideas of their own importance in the

[21] Daniel Dulany, *Considerations on the Propriety of Imposing Taxes on the American Colonies* (1765), p. 17.
[22] *Connecticut Courant,* Apr. 29, 1765; *Maryland Gazette,* Aug. 27, 1767, Feb. 22, 1770; *Pennsylvania Gazette,* Oct. 10, Nov. 7, 1771; etc.

empire and to their drive for economic and political autonomy.

The Americans were just in the process of finding themselves in the world: the French had been disposed of, for the time being; now the most important problem in the outside world for them was Britain. Gradually, in the course of the debates in the provincial assemblies and the Continental Congress, the continentals found themselves logically forced into the position that declared them to be sovereign states, at least internally.

As for the Anglo-French conflict, there was little thought about it in America between 1764 and 1774. As the tension with Britain approached the breaking point, however, the Americans began to re-discuss the old Anglo-French balance of power and they easily discovered the possibility of exploiting it for their own advantage. Franklin observed from London in 1769 and 1770 that all Europe was watching the dispute of Britain with her colonies and that sympathy was generally on the side of the colonies. At the same time, he said, "the malignant Pleasure, which other Powers take in British Divisions, may convince us on both sides of the Necessity of our uniting."[23] But the interest of Europe in the dispute, and particularly the interest of France, was soon recognized by the Americans as a possible trump in their own hand, rather than as a reason for compromising their difficulties with Britain.

It was John Adams who probably saw most clearly the potential value of the Anglo-French rivalry to the American cause; and although his first motion in the Continental Congress to send ambassadors abroad failed, he continued to argue for exploiting the Anglo-French enmity for the benefit of the embattled colonists. As he related it in his autobiography:

Some gentlemen doubted of the sentiments of France; thought she would frown upon us as rebels, and be afraid to countenance the example. I replied to those gentlemen, that I apprehended

[23] Benjamin Franklin, *The Writings of Benjamin Franklin*, ed. by Albert H. Smyth (10 vols., New York, 1905-1907), V, 254.

they had not attended to the relative situation of France and England; that it was the unquestionable interest of France that the British Continental Colonies should be independent; that Britain, by the conquest of Canada and her naval triumphs during the last war, and by her vast possessions in America and the East Indies, was exalted to a height of power and preëminence that France must envy and could not endure. But there was much more than pride and jealousy in the case. Her rank, her consideration in Europe, and even her safety and independence, were at stake.... that interest could not lie; that the interest of France was so obvious, and her motives so cogent, that nothing but a judicial infatuation of her councils could restrain her from embracing us; that our negotiations with France ought, however, to be conducted with great caution, and with all the foresight we could possibly obtain; that we ought not to enter into any alliance with her, which should entangle us in any future wars in Europe; that we ought to lay it down, as a first principle and maxim never to be forgotten, to maintain an entire neutrality in all future European wars; that it never could be our interest to unite with France in the destruction of England, or in any measures to break her spirit, or reduce her to a situation in which she could not support her independence. On the other hand, it could never be our duty to unite with Britain in too great a humiliation of France; that our real, if not our nominal, independence, would consist in our neutrality.... The opening of American trade to her [France], would be a vast resource for her commerce and naval power, and a great assistance to her in protecting her East and West India possessions, as well as her fisheries; but the bare dismemberment of the British empire would be to her an incalculable security and benefit, worth more than all the exertions we should require of her, even if it should draw her into another eight or ten years' war.[24]

So far had the weather vane of the American attitude shifted, between 1750 and 1775. The ancient enemy, France, for the description of whom in 1755 no language was powerful enough, no epithet scurrilous enough, was now become the prospective ally, to be courted for her aid; circumspectly and cautiously courted, to be sure, almost as a male black widow spider might court his deadly bride, but courted nonetheless. And for what?

[24] John Adams, *The Works of John Adams*, ed. by Charles F. Adams (10 vols., Boston, 1856), II, 503–506; quoted in E. C. Burnett, ed., *Letters of Members of the Continental Congress* (8 vols., Washington, 1921–36), I, 351 n.

To bring to realization the maturing sovereignty of the Anglo-American states. To give fruition to the drive for autonomy that had been in them for a century. It is of interest to observe that the basic concept of international affairs, for those who thought seriously on the subject, was still the concept of a mercantilistic balance of power—a balance in which the American colonies were thought to be the decisive makeweight. But the most significant fact that emerges from all the discussion, perhaps, is that the American people, divided though they were, were moving steadily and surely toward a national self-consciousness, though always, be it said, demanding only to be the first-born in a closely knit British family of autonomous states. The orientation of the slowly self-conscious American people toward the outside world was moving, in the years between 1750 and 1775, toward a demand for acceptance as a new member, or as a group of new members, albeit young and unproven, of the Atlantic community of nations.

THE IMPERIAL SCHOOL
OF AMERICAN COLONIAL HISTORIANS

T HE "imperial school of American colonial historians" may be
defined as that group of historians dealing with the British
colonies in the American hemisphere prior to 1783 whose fundamental approach to their subject is based upon the assumption
that, since those colonies were integral parts of the British
Empire, their history should be studied as the history of parts
of the Empire. This point of approach contrasts sharply with
that of the "nationalist" school of historians of the United
States, of which the most notable examples are perhaps George
Bancroft and John Fiske, and of which the most notable recent
exponent is Edward Channing—a school of historians who investigate the colonial period chiefly, if not exclusively, with the
objective of finding there the origins of the United States—of
which, of course, the British-Americans of the colonial period
never even dreamed! Thus, where the nationalist sees national
origins, the imperial historian sees the development of institutions within the framework and organic interrelationships of
that conglomerate aggregation of widely differing economic,
social, and political entities known as the "old British empire."
The nationalist historian sees the history of thirteen of these
many differing entities as something unique, for in it he finds

the origins and the foundations of a great nation; to the imperial historian, when he pushes his position to its logical conclusion, the so-called "thirteen" are merely some of the parts of a much larger phenomenon, the British Empire as a whole, which was itself only one of the major incidents in the expansion of European civilization round the world.

The first move among modern historians to write of the colonies from the point of view of the old Empire rather than from that of the new American nation came, naturally enough, in England itself. For there, men like George O. Trevelyan began to write of the colonies as communities of Englishmen, and of the American Revolution as a civil, rather than as an international war; and John A. Doyle, Fellow of All Souls College, Oxford, saw in the appearance of English communities in America chiefly, though not purely, the transition of culture form England to America. As he himself says in the introduction to his first volume, "I have preferred to regard the history of the United States as the transplantation of English ideas and institutions to a distant soil, and the adaptation of them to new wants and altered modes of life.... The history of the American colonies is in one sense nothing more than a continuation of English history.... The colonies did indeed one and all form for themselves institutions closely resembling those of the mother country. But these institutions were developed, not transplanted or servilely copied."[1]

It will be noted, here, that although Doyle sees the history of the United States as "the transplantation of English ideas and institutions," he anticipates, in the last sentence, the frontier theory of local variations just then being developed by Frederick Jackson Turner.

The study of the British overseas colonies of the old Empire has gone on apace in England since Trevelyan and Doyle, and the list of distinguished English colonial historians includes such

[1] John A. Doyle, *English Colonies in America* (5 vols., New York, 1889–1907), I, 1–2.

names as those of Sir John Seeley and James A. Williamson, and more recently, those of A. P. Newton and Richard Pares. One of the most distinguished products of this school is the recent first volume of the *Cambridge History of the British Empire*—a volume, indeed, that is apparently far too little known in this country.

It was easy and natural for Englishmen to write of the colonies as phenomena in the overseas expansion of Britain. It was not so easy for Americans, living in the shadow of George Bancroft and John Fiske, to throw off their nationalistic provincialism and bias and write of the colonies in the moods of the Englishmen and the British-Americans of the pre-Revolutionary era. Those American historians who managed it have introduced a new mood and a new perspective into American historiography.

The most notable American exponents of the imperial school of colonial historians are Herbert Levi Osgood, George Louis Beer, Charles McLean Andrews, and Lawrence Henry Gipson.

Osgood was the first important American historian of the colonial period to react against the narrow nationalistic bias of George Bancroft. A pupil of John W. Burgess, who was one of the major stars in the galaxy of German-trained, so-called "scientific" historians, Osgood was convinced that the colonial phase of American history should be studied as "a natural outgrowth of the history of Europe." Thus the task he set himself when he began his monumental study of the thirteen colonies in the seventeenth and eighteenth centuries was a twofold one. His own description of his effort is given in the preface to *The American Colonies in the Seventeenth Century* as follows: "The entire work, while serving as an introduction to American institutional history, will at the same time, it is hoped, illustrate the principles of British colonization, so far as those were revealed in the early relations between the home government and its colonies on the North American continent."[2]

2 Herbert L. Osgood, *The American Colonies in the Seventeenth Century* (3 vols., New York, 1904–1907), I, iii.

Thus on the one side, the origin and development of American institutions; on the other, the origin and development of British policy and the institutions of colonial administration and control; policy and institutions an understanding of which is so essential to any real understanding of the colonies and their history—or even of the history of the later United States, for that matter. But Osgood concerned himself only with the colonies on the continent of North America. His major interest was centered, after all, upon the origins of the institutions of the later United States. Thus while his perspective was a much broader one than that of his nationalistic predecessors, he assumed that it was unnecessary for him to concern himself with any of the British colonies other than the thirteen that eventually sceded from the Empire. Osgood is thus both an historian of the colonies and an historian of the United States. As Charles M. Andrews wrote of Osgood's history, it was "not British history, nor yet American history in any narrow and exclusive sense of that term, but something between, more American than British and growing more and more American with every decade that passes."[3]

The important thing about Osgood is that he realized, more than any other American historian of his generation, perhaps, the fact that the history of the British colonies in America in the eighteenth century could not be written without great error and distortion, even from the nationalistic point of view, without considering thoroughly and carefully what he called "the British side of the problem."

The realization of the second of Osgood's objectives, however, the examination of what he called "the British side of the problem," was not actually achieved by Osgood, but by one of his pupils, George Louis Beer. Beer, indeed, disclaimed any direct intention of writing any part of the history of the United States. As he put it, in the preface to his volume on *British Colonial*

[3] Quoted in Michael Kraus, *A History of American History* (New York, 1937), 422.

Policy, 1754-1765, this "is a study of British policy during the critical period of the old Empire. Thus the essay belongs distinctly to the domain of British history; but to the extent that English and American development were then inseparable, it also, but more indirectly, falls within the field occupied by American history. The focus of interest is, however, the British Empire, and not the rise of the American Nation."[4]

To Beer, then, his task was logically to investigate one aspect of the history of the British Empire. Any elucidation of the history of the United States that might result was for him purely coincidental. But he adhered conscientiously to the historical logic of his position, and his achievement is significant not merely because he made a major contribution to historical knowledge, but also because he succeeded in completely freeing himself from the bias of nationalism.

Charles M. Andrews, long the dean of the imperial school of American colonial historians and founder of a veritable school of distinguished students of the history of the colonial period among his own pupils, carried the logic of the "imperial" position forward to include all the British colonies in the American hemisphere. The title of his greatest work, *The Colonial Period of American History,* indicates that he, too, like Osgood, is still interested in United States origins; he simply feels that those origins can be seen and understood only in terms of *all* the British colonies in America, and of their relations with each other and with the mother country.

Thus, in the preface of his *magnum opus* he says: "I have had no intention of adding another account to the existing histories of the thirteen original colonies. I have been convinced for many years that to place the colonies in their rightful historical setting and so to discover what our colonial history is all about, it would be necessary to reëxamine the evidence from a vantage point other than that usually taken, to view them not

4 George L. Beer, *British Colonial Policy, 1754-1765* (New York, 1907), v.

from within, as is commonly done, but from without, with the movement constantly forward, following the natural course of historical development, and disregarding all preconceptions based on later events. For this purpose I have approached the subject from the English end, from the land whence the colonists came and of which they were always legally a part, and have broadened the scope of my inquiry to include all England's colonial possessions in the West that were founded in the seventeenth century. I have done this because I believe that final conclusions must always rest upon the experiences England had with all, not a part, of her colonies. That some of these colonies remained British while others became American does not, historically speaking, enter in as a determining factor."[5]

It is to be observed, of course, that Andrews' interest is still in the early period of "our history"—a phrase that he uses repeatedly. He is apparently at heart still a nationalist, just as Osgood was; his originality lay in his method of determining just what the truth in this early period of "our history" was. That is to say, he was convinced that any history of the "thirteen original colonies" that omitted a discussion of the British West Indies, on the one hand, or of the institutional development of the mother country relative to the colonies, on the other, could only result in a distortion of the truth. Thus to understand "our history," one must see this early part of it as an organic part of the British American Empire.

But Andrews succeeded in doing what neither Beer nor Osgood had succeeded in doing. For he was able to describe both the internal institutional developments of the colonies and the British institutions of colonial administration, together with the relationships between them, all together in his one great work.

But it is Lawrence H. Gipson who has carried the position of the Imperial School to its logical conclusion. For Gipson's

---

[5] Charles M. Andrews, *The Colonial Period of American History* (4 vols., New Haven, Connecticut, 1934–1938), I, xi.

work is concerned with the British Empire between 1750 and 1776 as such; and, except for the warm blast against Tom Paine, George Bancroft, and the historical distortions perpetrated by the nationalist school that appears in the beginning of volume six, Gipson writes his history much as a man of 1760 might have written it, as though the United States had never existed. He has succeeded, about as nearly as anyone might be expected to do, in divesting himself of the American habit of seeing the colonial period through the distorting haze of the history of the United States—even, indeed, of the "our history" mood of Andrews.

The title of Gipson's work indicates his position: *The British Empire Before the American Revolution.* His history, as it is projected, must, of course, include the history of the change in attitude on the part of the Americans of the thirteen colonies that led them, in the thirty-odd years before 1776, to change from contented British subjects into a body of Americans fired with a hatred of England and determined upon independence. But Gipson's work is, nevertheless, primarily a history of the old Empire in that period. And, since it is that, it is not limited to the colonies in the American hemisphere, but includes all the colonies of the Empire, including those of Africa and India; further, as it is a history of the Empire as a whole and not just the colonies, it must needs discuss all the other parts of the Empire as well, including Britain itself. Gipson begins about 1750; for, as he says, "to get a view of the old Empire in a state of tranquillity and equilibrium for the last time in its history one must indeed turn to the brief period between the end of the War of the Austrian Succession and the outbreak of hostilities between the English and French in North America that led to the great Seven Years' War."[6]

Thus Gipson is primarily and exclusively an historian of the

[6] Lawrence H. Gipson, *The British Empire Before the American Revolution* (6 vols., Caldwell, Idaho, and New York, 1936–1946), I, *Great Britain and Ireland*, viii.

old British Empire. The problem he sets himself is much broader than that of either Osgood, Beer, or Andrews; his approach to history is much broader, also; for where they are historians of institutions, Gipson is an historian of civilization, covering social phenomena, military and economic history, and other aspects of life as well as political events and institutions. He is concerned little, if at all, with the history of the United States, although he does give a little greater emphasis to the American British colonies than he does to the British colonies elsewhere in the world, and although in any discussion of imperial history in the years between 1750 and 1775 the reasons for the American Revolution and the formation of the United States must inevitably appear.

These, then, are the chief American exponents of the imperial school of colonial historians. Osgood, Beer, and Andrews appear to belong, in the last analysis, to the so-called German school of "scientific" history. Their works are all primarily institutional histories; and all three of these writers, particularly Beer and Andrews, base their conclusions largely upon original source materials of an "official" documentary sort. As Andrews says, "The historian, if he is to keep both his levels and his proportions true, cannot fail to stress, first of all, the institutional and structural aspects of colonial life, which, despite certain present-day opinions to the contrary, are fundamental to any right understanding of the colonial past."[7] Gipson, on the other hand, is more of a social historian. As he says, his work "makes no attempt to institutionalize the old British Empire but is concerned rather with an analysis of some of those forces—economic, social, and political—motivating various geographical groups within it before the American Revolution."[8] His work, too, is based predominantly upon official documents; but he uses more contemporary imprints and personal papers than the others.

[7] Andrews, *The Colonial Period of American History*, IV, 428.
[8] Gipson, *The British Empire Before the American Revolution*, I, ix.

All of these historians are conscious of, and affected by, the influence of economic concerns upon human history. As Andrews says, however, "if he [the historian] is honest to himself and his evidence he cannot neglect the imponderable forces (always most difficult to identify and trace), as well as the driving influence of emotional and mass psychology. These factors are essential, however much those who can see in society, present and past, only things that are 'real' and 'practical' ... and consider irrelevant whatever cannot be pinned down as a social or economic activity. No one should deal with the past whose ambition it is to find a single cause for all that has happened or who is unwilling to admit the existence of many causes acting simultaneously."[9] He quotes J. M. Keynes to the effect that " 'The view that the economic ideal is the sole respectable purpose of the community as a whole is the most dreadful heresy which has ever gained the ear of a civilized people.' "[10] And Andrews himself continues, "Modern industrialism would seem to be responsible for these latter-day attempts to interpret the past in the light of the present and to apply the Marxian doctrine that social progress is the outcome of class conflict and of nothing else."[11]

It is of considerable interest to notice that, with the exception of Beer, the historians of this group share some of the basic positions of the so-called "frontier school" of American historians symbolized by Frederick Jackson Turner. For Osgood, Andrews, and Gipson all appear to accept, in one degree or another, the proposition that the culture inherited from the mother country underwent so profound a modification or differentiation in the course of replanting and new growth in the new environment as to make the product of this adaptation an essentially new variant of the broad culture pattern of western civilization. Andrews describes the colonies in the eighteenth century as

[9] Andrews, *The Colonial Period of American History*, IV, 428.
[10] *Ibid.*
[11] *Ibid.*

having "marked individual and sectional differences that made coöperation difficult and union practically impossible, each moving forward in its own sphere toward a popular and local management of its own affairs, through the growth to prominence and leadership of its representative assembly. These colonies . . . were putting into practice certain ideas regarding government, law, land tenure, and finance that were not in accord with English precedent and usage. In these conflicts and divergences of the eighteenth century are to be found the beginnings of American history properly so called. . . ."[12] And in another place Andrews says, "The story of how this was done—how that which was English slowly and imperceptibly merged into that which was American—has never been adequately told; but it is a fascinating phase of history, more interesting and enlightening when studied against the English background than when construed as an American problem only. It is the story of the gradual elimination of those elements, feudal and proprietary, that were foreign to the normal life of a frontier land, and of the gradual adjustment of the colonies to the restraints and restrictions that were imposed upon them by the commercial policy of the mother country. It is the story also of the growth of the colonial assemblies. . . . It is above all . . . the story of the gradual transformation of these assemblies from the provincial councils that the home government intended them to be into miniature parliaments. At the end of a long struggle . . . they emerged powerful legislative bodies, as self-conscious in their way as the House of Commons in England was becoming during the same eventful years."[13] On the other hand, in seeing the emergence of truly American institutions, differentiated from those of England or of Europe under the influence of the local American geographic and ethnic environment as manifestations

[12] *Ibid.*, I, xiii.
[13] C. M. Andrews, "The American Revolution: An Interpretation," *American Historical Review*, XXXI (1925-1926), 226-227.

of the Turnerian process in the formation of cultures, these historians in effect relate the Turner thesis to the larger process of European expansion. The result seems to be that the American frontier becomes the frontier of western civilization, to be sure, but one in which both the processes of continuity and the processes of new cultural growth are going on together to produce, around the periphery of the so-called Atlantic community, cultures which are, to say the very least, new and in many cases sharply different cultural variants of western civilization. Further, as the history of the "old British empire" is a part of the expansion of Europe in general, these historians, particularly Beer, Osgood, and Gipson, along with Francis Parkman, relate the development of the British colonies, in one way or another, to the parallel developments of their non-British neighbors; although it is Herbert E. Bolton and his students who have made the most conscious and deliberate efforts to relate the Anglo-Saxon colonial expansion in this hemisphere to that of the other colonizing European nations.

The broadened perspective of the imperial school of colonial historians, and their effort to see the British-American colonial phenomenon in terms of its organic relationship with Britain and the rest of the Empire, seems to be a refutation, for this particular group, at least, of Professor C. J. H. Hayes' charge at Washington that "a striking general fact about it [our historical writing] during the past seventy years has been the tendency to turn away from European themes and to concentrate upon strictly American."[14] This generalization is probably in a general sense true. And it is also doubtless true, as Professor Hayes says, that the vogue of the restricted interpretation of the American frontier that sees it as "a peculiarly American phenomenon, determining the unique character of our national society and culture," and "the concurrent neglect of broader and other-

[14] Carlton J. H. Hayes, "The American Frontier—Frontier of What?" *American Historical Review*, LI (1945–1946), 202.

wise obvious considerations, have been . . . at once a result and a stimulant of growing intellectual isolationism in the United States."[15]

But the members of the imperial school have been acutely conscious of the provincialism of historians of the United States in their approach to the colonial period, and they deliberately set out to combat it. To quote Andrews again, "American writers except in an incidental way, have ignored the English side of the story, because it was English and therefore out of their range if not beyond their ken. . . . The time must come, however, when this duality of interest will be regarded as a necessary part of the stock in trade of every serious writer on the subject who deals with it in a fair-minded and comprehensive way, and not until that time has come will this long and eventful period of our country's past receive its merited treatment as history unalloyed and find proper recognition not merely as a phase preliminary to our own career as a nation, but also as an integral part of the English and Continental history in an era of colonization and commercial and maritime aggrandizement."[16]

Gipson is even more deliberate in his effort to correct the errors of provincial American nationalism. As he puts it in the preface to Volume VI of his monumental description of the British Empire before the American Revolution, "In the present work one of the motives that dictated the selection of topics and space allotted to each of these has been a desire to emphasize certain important aspects of the history of this conflict [The Seven Years' War] that have been, it would seem, especially subject to popular misconceptions and even to serious misinterpretations on the part of many historians and of others who are not."[17] And among the chief of these misconceptions, fathered

15 *Ibid.*, 201.
16 Andrews, *The Colonial Period of American History*, I, xiv.
17 Gipson, *The British Empire Before the American Revolution*, VI, *The Great War For the Empire*, ix.

by Tom Paine and propagated by George Bancroft, was the idea "that the connection of Americans with monarchical Great Britain, far from being a blessing, had actually been a curse. . . ."[18]

The imperial school of colonial historians, then, may be said to be distinguished by its deliberate effort to relate what was going on in British America in the seventeenth and eighteenth centuries to what was going on in Europe at the same time, thereby placing the history of this continent in a more correct perspective relative to the development of western civilization as a whole. While they do seem to accept, if with some caution, the Turner hypothesis of the formation of new cultures, they relate that hypothesis to the great phenomenon, the expansion of Europe. In doing so it would appear that they, perhaps more than any other group of historians interested primarily in American history, have escaped the limitations of nationalistic bias or myopia. It might even be suggested that an attitude toward American history, or any part of it, that sees that history in terms of its world perspective is highly desirable in a generation of historians as acutely conscious as ours is that our very survival as a nation seems to depend upon an understanding of the origins and nature of our external relations.

[18] *Ibid.*, 5.

NATIONALISM AND OTHER LOYALTIES
IN THE AMERICAN REVOLUTION

Loyalties of one sort or another have always been powerful causal forces in human history. It was the personal loyalty of the vassal to his lord that gave to medieval feudalism its cohesive force; it is individual and collective loyalty to the nation which, today, holds the national societies of the modern world together. This peculiar form of loyalty did not become a major factor in the history of the Western world until about the middle of the eighteenth century. Nor could it have been until the concept of the nation had become a reality in the ideologies of Western societies since nationalism is a form of loyalty whose object is the nation.

But what is a nation? No one has ever seen a nation; no one has ever touched one. The nation has no existence in the physical world. Its existence, therefore, while nonetheless real, is entirely metaphysical, or mental; the nation exists only as a concept held in common by many men. It is the emotional loyalty of men to this always changing concept, the nation, that constitutes nationalism. Without the concept, the loyalty could not exist.

The concept of the nation appeared in the Western world apparently as a by-product of the emergence of the modern integral state. One of those who, as it were, first seized upon the mental image of the nation was Jean Jacques Rousseau, who stated it clearly in his "Considerations sur le gouvernement de Pologne . . . ," when he said, "A child on opening its eyes for the first time should see the nation, and until death he should see nothing but her. Every true national imbibes with his mother's milk the love of *la patrie*. . . . This love encompasses his entire existence; he sees only the nation, he lives only for her; alone, he is nothing; the moment he is without the nation he ceases to exist. . . ."[1]

Lord Bolingbroke skirted the same concept in his essay on "The Idea of a Patriot King" and elsewhere,[2] and Edmund Burke apparently had in mind a clear concept of the British nation—a nation he was trying desperately to hold together—when he made his famous plea for reconciliation with the colonies on March 22, 1775:

> My hold of the Colonies is in the close affection which grows from common names, from kindred blood, from similar privileges, and equal protection. These are ties, which, though light as air, are as strong as links of iron. Let the Colonists always keep the idea of their civil rights associated with your government;—they will cling and grapple to you; and no force under heaven will be of power to tear them from their allegiance. . . . Deny them this participation of freedom, and you break that sole bond, which originally made, and must still preserve, the unity of the Empire. . . . It is the spirit of the English Constitution, which, infused through the mighty mass, pervades, feeds, unites, invigorates, unifies every part of the empire, even down to the minutest member. . . .[3]

It is to be noted that the concept of the British nation and of loyalty to it, here appealed to by Burke, was expressed in the term "the Empire." This term was also used by the Americans down to

[1] Jean Jacques Rousseau, "Considerations sur le gouvernement de Pologne et sur sa reformation projetée en avril 1772" (printed in J. J. Rousseau, *Contrat Social, ou Principes du Droit Politique* . . . [Paris, n.d.], 356).

[2] Henry St. John, Viscount Bolingbroke, *Letters on the Spirit of Patriotism: On the Idea of a Patriot King: and On the State of Parties, At the Accession of King George the First* (London, 1749), *passim*.

[3] *Burke: Select Works*, ed. E. J. Payne (3 vols., Oxford, Eng., 1904), I, 231–32.

1776, and it was borrowed, as "the American Empire," to indicate the American nation as that new concept grew in the minds of Americans after independence. The psychological, the emotional cement that bound together the members of the British nation wherever they were was for Burke and other British nationalists the English mythos, the central, essential element in which was the belief in the reality of an Anglo-Saxon love of liberty.

The Britons of Anglo-America shared in this Burkean type of nationalism. They gloried in the name of Briton, and they felt a genuine emotional identity with this concept of the British nation. William Douglass, for example, expressed this American-British loyalty in his *Summary, Historial and Political ... of the British Settlements in North-America:* "The high encomiums of our militia ought not to give any umbrage or jealousy to the British government or mother-country; that in case of any general (maritime powers) war, they cast themselves into the arms of the French or Dutch; ... the people here [Massachusetts] are so loyal to the crown, and so affectionate to their mother country, that this cannot be supposed...."[4] Benjamin Franklin echoed this sense of common nationalism during the Seven Years' War as he wrote to Lord Kames in January 1760: "No one can more sincerely rejoice than I do, on the reduction of Canada; and this is not merely as I am a colonist, but as I am a Briton...."[5] A little later in the same year, in his famous pamphlet on "Guadaloupe" [*sic*], he made his British nationalism sharply clear when he remarked that "if ever there was a *national war*, this is truly such a one: a war in which the interest of the *whole* nation is directly and fundamentally concerned."[6]

This feeling of "affection" for the mother country persisted into

[4] William Douglass, *A Summary, Historical and Political, of the First Planting, Progressive Improvements, and Present State of the British Settlements in North-America* (2 vols., Boston, 1755), I, 7.

[5] *The Writings of Benjamin Franklin*, ed. Albert H. Smyth (10 vols., New York, 1905-1907), IV, 4.

[6] *Ibid.*, 51. The italics are Franklin's.

the years of crisis, right down to the eve of independence, in the minds and feelings of both American Whigs and American Tories. It ended, for the Whigs, with independence; it continued to dominate the thought and feeling of the Tories through and beyond the Revolution.

Yet the Americans distinctly felt themselves to be different from other Britons, and in many ways. Jonathan Mayhew, celebrating the triumph of British arms in the Seven Years' War, enumerated the peculiar satisfactions of being a member of the British nation: "We Britishers are still farther distinguished and favoured of God, by having been born and bred in a *protestant* country, and a *reformed* part of the christian church...."[7] But if it was a peculiar privilege to be born a member of the British nation, this special favor of God reached superlative heights in one's being born a Britisher of New England. "If we come to our own country in particular; we have here enjoyed, of late, almost all the blessings of peace, in a time of war and tumult among the nations of Europe...."[8] Mayhew, in speaking of "our own country," as his contemporaries were accustomed to do, had in mind his native New England. He was proud to be a Briton, and he loved the ideals that, to him, made the British nation the happiest and best in the world. But it was the "New-English" Britons who enjoyed, more than any other, the national values, the most precious of which were the civil rights and privileges that were theirs as members of the British nation.

It was this coupling of a sense of identity with the British nation with a distinct consciousness of differentness and a certain smug self-satisfaction in it that characterized the "British" nationalism of the colonial Americans. The citizen of any one of the colonies looked upon that colony as his "country," and he felt a distinct patriotism, or love of his land, toward it. Some of the colonists even spoke of "America" as the aggregate of the colonies,

[7] Jonathan Mayhew, *Two Sermons* (Boston, 1763), 17–72.
[8] *Ibid.*, 73.

and betrayed, on numerous occasions, an active and enthusiastic sense of the "manifest destiny" (to use a later phrase) of the American segment of the British nation.[9]

This consciousness of being a different sort of Briton living in a different "country" was apparently a strong germinal factor in the origin and, later, the emergence of a self-conscious American nationalism. In the years following the Seven Years' War it enjoyed a new burst of enthusiastic, emotional expression. But this feeling for one's "country" (colony) and for America in a collective or pluralistic sense was always focused upon the new land only within the larger context of the Empire. The colonial Americans were never less than loyal to their nation—the nation of Britons everywhere; their loyalties to America were always subservient to and integrated in their greater loyalty to the "Empire" and its ideals.

II

The history of loyalties in Anglo-America in the years between 1763 and 1775 is not one of divided loyalties, but, rather, a history of two separate, distinct, and rival series of efforts to preserve the old American loyalty to the British nation. The American Whigs stood for the maintenance of the old loyalty to the British national ideals, as they understood them, *against* the policies and actions of what they took to be a series of misguided ministries; the Tories clung to the old loyalty *despite* the policies of those same ministries, however misguided. For the Tories, as contrasted with the Whigs or Radicals, British national symbols, ideals, and loyalties in the Burkean sense were everything. If worse came to worst, they would submit to the ministry rather than split the British nation and precipitate it into civil war. The Whigs always maintained

9 For an example of this American sense of manifest destiny, see Nathaniel Ames's *Astronomical Diary* (Boston, 1757) for 1758. For a discussion of the early American idea of manifest destiny, see John C. Parrish, *The Emergence of the Idea of Manifest Destiny* (Los Angeles, 1932).

that their loyalty to the British nation, and to the crown as its symbol, was just as strong and devoted as that of any other Britons, and they demonstrated their sincerity in their writings. John Dickinson, for example, in the midst of American fury over the Townshend program, betrayed a deep emotional fear of a rending of the "body" of the British nation:

> Resistance, in the case of colonies against their mother country, is extremely different from the resistance of a people against their prince. A nation may change their king, or race of kings, and ... be gainers by changing. ... But if once we [the colonies] are separated from our mother country, what new form of government shall we adopt, or where shall we find another Britain, to supply our loss? Torn from the body to which we are united by religion, liberty, laws, affections, relation, language and commerce, we must bleed at every vein.[10]

A few years later, Samuel Adams, in his debate with Thomas Hutchinson, pointed out that all the American Whigs insisted upon was some sort of constitutional reform that would ensure to the Americans the same constitutional guarantees that the Britons living in England enjoyed. Given this guarantee, he said, the loyalty of the Americans to the British-imperial national ideal would remain true and undiminished.[11] Persistent wrongheadedness by English ministers might destroy American loyalty to the "Empire," but enlightened constitutional reform—even just the honest recognition and institutionalization of the real *status quo* —might be expected to preserve and encourage American loyalty to the national ideal indefinitely.

A similar effort to fit the expediency of constitutional reform into a generally received concept of and loyalty to the British imperial nation is to be observed in the writings of John Adams in 1774 and 1775. In the first of his *Novanglus* essays, for example,

---

[10] *Writings of John Dickinson*, ed. Paul L. Ford (14 vols., Philadelphia, 1895), I, 169.

[11] *The Writings of Samuel Adams*, ed. Harry A. Cushing (3 vols., New York, 1906), II, 424 *et passim*.

Adams introduced his series of replies to Massachusettensis (Daniel Leonard) with: "A writer, under the signature of Massachusettensis, has addressed you, in a series of papers, on the great national subject of the present quarrel between the British administration and the Colonies."[12] Adams here used the term "national" to indicate the totality of British imperial society. He recognized clearly the fact that there were two segments of that society, the English and the American, but the whole British national society on both sides of the Atlantic was one, and he was loyal to it.[13] It is a notable fact that Leonard's concept of the British nation was basically the same as that of Adams. Their difference arose chiefly over Adams' insistence that the Americans were entitled to different, special treatment as Britons, a treatment that could be administered only by their own colonial governments and some sort of continental congress.

Thomas Jefferson, evidently, was thinking along similar lines. In his "Draft of Instructions to the Virginia Delegates in the Continental Congress" of July 1774, he proposed a "humble and dutiful address" to the King, presenting the strong American discontents on the encroachments of "the legislature of one part of the empire, upon those rights which God and the laws have given equally and independently to all."[14] And in the Resolution of the Virginia Convention of August 1774, the Virginians avowed their

> ... inviolable and unshaken fidelity and attachment to our most gracious Sovereign, our Regard and affection for all our Friends and Fellow Subjects in Great Britain and elsewhere, [and protest] against every Act or Thing which may have the most distant ten-

[12] John Adams and Jonathan Sewall (*sic*) [John Adams, as editor, was mistaken; the author of the Massachusettensis papers was Daniel Leonard], *Novanglus and Massachusettensis, or Political Essays, published in the Years 1774 and 1775, On the Principal Points of Controversy, between Great Britain and Her Colonies* (Boston, 1819), 9.

[13] *Ibid.*, 26, 27–29, 30–31, *et passim.*

[14] *The Papers of Thomas Jefferson*, ed. Julian P. Boyd *et al.* (15 vols., Princeton, N. J., 1950–   ), I, 121.

dency to interrupt, or in any wise disturb, his Majesty's Peace, and the good Order of Government within this his ancient Colony, which we are resolved to maintain and defend at the Risk of our Lives and Fortunes....[15]

This was not the language of American nationalism. It was British nationalism. And the Virginians surely meant what they said.

James Wilson expressed similar sentiments.[16] He asked, after a review of American resistance, "Are these measures, Sir, the brats of disloyalty, of disaffection? . . . [No!] Is this scheme of conduct allied to rebellion? Can any symptoms of disloyalty to his Majesty, of disinclination to his illustrious family, or of disregard to his authority be traced in it?"[17] No. American opposition to the mistaken measures of the ministry was entirely constitutional; the Americans had never shown disloyalty "to his Majesty"; they were not "enemies to the power of the crown."[18] Alexander Hamilton said much the same thing in his dispute with the Westchester Farmer (Samuel Seabury): "I deny that we are dependent on the legislature of Great Britain; and yet I maintain that we are a part of the British Empire—but in this sense only, as being the free-born subjects of his Britannic Majesty."[19] John Hancock, on March 5, 1774, cried out for "patriotism" against the tyranny of British ministers. Like Wilson, he applauded the steps that had been taken to organize the colonies in a federated common front against the actions of an unwise ministry, steps that he hoped might culminate in a congress of all the continental colonies:

At such a congress a firm foundation may be laid for the security of our rights and liberties [,] a system may be formed for our common safety, by a strict adherence to which, we shall be able to

[15] *Ibid.,* 137.
[16] *The Works of James Wilson,* ed. James de Witt Anderson (2 vols., Chicago, 1896), II, 553 *et passim.*
[17] *Ibid.,* 563.
[18] *Ibid.*
[19] *The Works of Alexander Hamilton,* ed. Henry C. Lodge (12 vols., New York and London, 1904), I, 86.

frustrate any attempts to overthrow our constitution; restore peace and harmony to America, and secure honor and wealth to Great Britain, even against the inclination of her ministers, whose duty it is to study her welfare. . . .[20]

Even as late as November 4, 1775, the council of the town of Watertown, Massachusetts, issued a "Proclamation of Thanksgiving" urging the people of the town to render up thanks for their liberties and for the union of the colonies to defend them, "and to offer up humble and fervent prayers to Almighty God, for the whole British empire; especially for the *United American Colonies:*— . . . that He would give wisdom to the American Congress equal to their important station. . . ."[21]

Finally, the Continental Congress, itself, was still protesting its loyalty in July 1775:

> Attached to your Majesty's person, family, and government, with all devotion that principle and affection can inspire, connected with Great Britain by the strongest ties that can unite societies, and deploring every event that tends in any degree to weaken them, we solemnly assure your Majesty that we not only most ardently desire the former harmony between her and these colonies may be restored, but that a concord may be established between them upon so firm a basis as to perpetuate its blessings, uninterrupted by any future dissensions, to succeeding generations in both countries. . . .[22]

Surely there is no reason to think that these men in the colonies did not believe what they said. They did mean it, apparently; there is even a sort of pathos in their repeated and fervent protestations, as though they deeply feared to lose a connection with the British nation which, to them, was a highly precious thing.

Philip Freneau, the greatest poet of the revolutionary era, put into poetic language his own nostalgia for the good old days of national unity, late in 1775, in his poem "A Voyage to Boston";

[20] *Principles and Acts of the Revolution in America* . . . , ed. Hezekiah Niles (Baltimore, 1822), 42.

[21] *Ibid.*, 125.

[22] *Journals of the Continental Congress, 1774–1789*, ed. W. C. Ford *et al.* (34 vols., Washington, D.C., 1904–37), II, 161.

O Britain come, and, if you can, relent
This rage, that better might on Spain be spent.
....

Long may Britannia rule our hearts again,
Rule as she rul'd in George The Second's reign;
May ages hence her growing empire see,
And she be glorious, but ourselves be free,
In that just scale an equal balance hold,
And grant these climes a second age of gold.[23]

The evidence thus appears to be overwhelming that, at least
until late 1775, there was no significant split in the loyalties of
the Americans. All Americans, Whigs and Tories alike, were
genuinely and deeply loyal to the "British empire" or nation, to
its ideals, and to its king. The divisions among them were divisions as to practical constitutional reforms, their validity and
their importance, not as to national British ideals or loyalty to
those ideals.

III

Evidently, the British national loyalty of the Anglo-Americans
was real. Their concept of the "empire" was one of the nation of
Britons wherever they were, on both sides of the Atlantic or elsewhere. Yet the Americans' sense of differentness and their consciousness that they were a peculiar and specially favored segment
of this imperial society were equally real and were growing with
great intensity. It was this sense of a special destiny within the
Empire that inspired William Livingston to exclaim, in 1770, in
his poem *America,*

Hail Land of light and joy! Thy power shall grow
Far as the seas, which round thy regions flow:
Through earth's wide realms thy glory shall extend,
And savage nations at thy scepter bend.[24]

[23] *The Poems of Philip Freneau,* ed. Fred L. Pattee (3 vols., Princeton, N.J.,
1902–1907), I, 161, 181.
[24] William Livingston, *America: or, a Poem on the Settlement of the
British Colonies; Addressed to the Friends of Freedom, and Their Country*
(New Haven, Conn., 1770), 11.

John Trumbull predicted a future glory and cultural leadership for America: "America hath a fair prospect in a few centuries of ruling both in arts and arms. It is universally allowed that we very much excell in the force of natural genius: And although but few among us are able to devote their whole lives to study, perhaps there is no nation in which a larger portion of learning is diffused through all ranks of people. . . ."[25] And he continued in poetic vein:

> See, this blest land in orient morn appears.
>
> ....
>
> In radiant state th' imperial realm shall rise,
> Her splendor circling to the boundless skies;
> Of every Fair she boasts the assembled charms,
> The Queen of empires and the nurse of arms.[26]

Philip Freneau and Hugh Henry Brackenridge sang the same sort of glorious future for America at the Princeton commencement of 1771:

> Hail, happy land,
> The seat of empire, the abode of kings,
> The final stage where time shall introduce
> Renowned characters, and glorious works
> Of high invention and of wond'rous art
> Which not the ravages of time shall waste
> Till he himself has run his long career.[27]

It was as though every poet with a pen and an impulse to write found the glory and manifest destiny of America the most magnificent and challenging theme to his muse. Even the Tories felt the same enthusiasm for this favored segment of the imperial society. Joseph Galloway, for example, elaborated upon the future of this, "my country," in terms that sound very much like

[25] John Trumbull, *The Use and Advantages of the Fine Arts* (New Haven, Conn., 1770), 11–12.

[26] *The Poetical Works of John Trumbull, LL.D.* (2 vols., Hartford, Conn., 1820), II, 158.

[27] "The Rising Glory of America," in *Poems of Philip Freneau*, ed. Pattee, I, 82, 83.

an American nationalism.[28] Yet it never occurred to any of these American patriots that this great future lay outside the body of the British imperial society or nation.

It is an arresting fact that the American Tories, in the period prior to 1776, were in no essential way different from the Whigs in their fundamental loyalties. As opponents of the Radicals, they differed from them chiefly on the nature of constitutional reform and on the question of how far proposed revisions of the imperial constitution could go without endangering the fabric of the Empire.

It was upon this point that Thomas Hutchinson reached an impasse in his debate with Samuel Adams. He identified nation and state, as so many Tories did. For him, a division of political authority such as Adams proposed would be tantamount to a splitting of the nation—a situation which was, to him, unthinkable: "His Majesty considers the British Empire as one entire Dominion, subject to one Supreme Legislative Power, a due submission to which is essential to the Maintenance of the Rights, Liberties and Privileges of the several Parts of this Dominion...."[29] Many Tories, indeed, could not divest themselves of the fear that the spiritual fabric and unity of the nation would be rent by political federalism, and they could see no other, larger perspective.

To certain other Tories such, for example, as Daniel Leonard, the errors of the ministries were hardly less egregious than they were to Radicals like John Adams. But Leonard feared both a split in the national unity and a release of the irresponsible passions of the mob. Yet his devotion to the concept of the British nation was almost identical with that held by many American Whigs, and he quoted John Dickinson to prove it.[30]

[28] Joseph Galloway, *A Candid Examination of the Mutual Claims of Great Britain and the Colonies: with a Plan of Accommodation, on Constitutional Principles* (New York, 1775), 34–36, 53, 54, *et passim*.
[29] Thomas Hutchinson, *The Speeches of His Excellency Governor Hutchinson to the General Assembly of the Massachusetts Bay* (Boston, 1773), 84.
[30] Adams and Leonard, *Novanglus and Massachusettensis*, 184-85.

Galloway, who ultimately made the great decision to cleave to his loyalty to the ideals of the British Empire, was not afraid to contemplate a constitutional reform that was curiously similar to, but in ways more radical and far reaching than those being proposed by John Adams and John Hancock. Galloway, probably the most profound of all the American Tory thinkers, identified state and nation, and he quoted Jean Jacques Burlamaqui to the effect that "The state is a body, or society animated by *one soul,* which directs *all its motions,* and makes *all its members* act after a *constant and uniform manner,* with a view to one and the same end, namely the *public* utility."[31] For Galloway, the British Empire, including "both countries" (Britain and America), was such a state-nation. The supreme authority in the imperial society was the king, who represented the whole state. But the British imperial society was clearly a nation composed of two countries, Britain and America—"my country." Americans had a right to a parliament of their own, and Galloway warned Britain that

> No people in the world have higher notions of liberty. It would be impossible to eradicate them.... [America's distance from England, its vast territory, its great commerce, its increasing strength and power] all point out the policy of uniting the two countries together, upon principles of English liberty—should this be omitted, the Colonies will infallibly throw off their connexion with the Mother Country....[32]

Daniel Dulany, another Tory, criticized the mother country in similar vein, and betrayed a comparable American patriotism. He recommended that Americans turn to manufactures: "Let it be demonstrated that the subjects of the *British* Empire in *Europe* and *America* are the same, that the Hardships of the latter will ever recoil upon the former."[33] His is a sort of economic nation-

[31] Quoted in Galloway, *Candid Examination,* 11.
[32] *Ibid.,* 53, 54.
[33] Daniel Dulany, *Considerations on the Propriety of Imposing Taxes in the British Colonies, for the Purpose of Raising a Revenue, by Act of Parliament* (North America [*sic*], 1765), 46.

alism; the concept of the nation that it exhibits is one that brackets "British subjects" on both sides of the Atlantic in a common national society.

Hamilton's great antagonist, Samuel Seabury, expressed another facet of Tory loyalty. He attacked the "new and shallow Heresy," that the American colonials owed their supreme loyalty (or allegiance) to the king, but not to Parliament, and he argued, on the basis of expediency, for a strong central authority. But he actually proposed such a constitutional reform as might provide for colonial autonomy without surrendering the sovereignty of Parliament. Like Hutchinson, Seabury could not see the possibility, that Hamilton had suggested, of having practically sovereign colonial governments, internally, without splitting the fabric of the British nation. Given the kind of constitutional reform that he, Seabury, proposed, the colonies would be relieved of too great a dependence upon Parliament, "and the mother country and all her colonies will be knit together in one grand, firm, and compact body."[34] In Seabury's mind the supreme consideration was "the honor, splendor, and majesty of the British Empire." As so many of his contemporaries, he was clearly using this term to indicate the British nation. Here, too, was the nationalism of an American born and bred. But it was a British nationalism.

One more example of British-American Tory national feeling may be cited—John Randolph. His "country," Virginia, was in distress: it was at once threatened by the ravages of the savage Indians at the rear and rent by the tensions of dispute with the mother country. Speaking of the necessity for unity in support of the government of Virginia against the Indians, Randolph said, "I have frequently heard the term Patriotism mentioned. . . . True Patriotism consists not in a separate attachment to any particular Branch, but in the Preservation of the several Parts of Government in that Degree of strength and vigour which the

[34] Samuel Seabury, *A View of the Controversy* (New York, 1774), 23.

Constitution intends that each shall enjoy. . . ."[35] "Patriotism"
was a loyalty toward Virginia.

As for the tensions between the colonies and England, Randolph made this amazing prediction and plea for British national
unity:

> The Histories of dependent states put it beyond a doubt that
> America, when she is able to protect herself, will acknowledge no
> Superiority in another. That she will be capable, some time or
> other, to establish an Independence, must appear evident to every
> one, who is acquainted with her present situation and growing
> strength. . . .[36]

If England persevered in its unwarranted rigor toward the colonies, "the Parent will soon be without a Child, and the Offspring
become unable to support itself":

> [America] is a great Country, and wants nothing to bring it to
> Perfection but Numbers. . . .
>
> A more pleasing and natural Connection never subsisted between
> any different Bodies of Men than did till of late, . . . between *Great
> Britain* and her Colonies. The Americans are descended from the
> Loins of *Britons,* and therefore may, with Propriety, be called the
> Children, and *England* the Mother of them. We are not only allied
> by Blood, but are still farther united, by the extensive Trade and
> Commerce carried on between us. Our Manners are similar; our
> Religion, and Language, the same. . . .[37]

This might have been Dickinson, or Galloway, or even Burke.
Randolph's plea was one of the most eloquent statements of
British nationalism by Anglo-Americans. Indeed, it was the
Tories such as Hutchinson, Seabury, Leonard, Galloway, Dulany,
and Randolph who were the true nationalists in the years before
1776. To them, the nation, the British nation, was real, and the
concept of it, its image, was supreme, vivid, and commanding in
their minds and hearts. And for this nation, its mythos, its ideals.

[35] John Randolph, *Considerations on the State of Virginia* (n.p., 1774).
17–18.
[36] *Ibid.,* 21–22.
[37] *Ibid.,* 23. 24.

and its present majesty, they were willing to sacrifice property, status, life itself, if need be.

IV

But if Radical and Tory were both British nationalists, differing chiefly as to the need and the nature of constitutional reform and not in their basic loyalties to the nation and its symbols, the logic of the course of events was driving them further and further apart in their reactions to expediency, and ever nearer to the break from beyond which there could be no return: the final abandonment, by the Whigs, of their long-persevering loyalty to the British nation and their consequent search for new concepts and new symbols toward which to direct new loyalties.

Despite the fundamental assumption of both the earliest colonial entrepreneurs and the crown that the American colonial societies were but extensions of the society of England, *de facto* British colonial policy, almost from the beginning, had treated them as somehow different and separate. Wisdom, in the handling of the colonial problem, had seemed to dictate a special set of laws to channel colonial commerce and limit colonial manufactures, special regulations affecting internal colonial affairs such as postal service, fiscal affairs, and military defense, special instructions to colonial governors to administer their duties in ways that differed widely, in some aspects, from the functioning of analogous political mechanisms in England, and so on. This old set of legal and *de facto* assumptions as to the differentness of the colonies and the consequent necessity for special laws and institutions for their administration underlay the whole series of ministerial colonial programs in the sixteen years preceding independence, and it reached its culmination in the American Prohibitory Act of December 22, 1775, by which the Americans of the thirteen continental colonies were declared to be enemies of England and were ordered to be treated as such. As the climax of a centuries-long series of *voies de fait,* this act was something like childbirth, actually forcing the offspring out of the body of the parent.

Nor had the Americans failed to be conscious of the fact that the colonial societies were, in very truth, highly different from that of the mother country. They had steadily grown toward the conviction that they alone could understand their internal problems and that, therefore, the mother country must recognize the sort of autonomy they were separately demanding and the sort of federative principle of empire being expounded, between 1765 and 1774, by Richard Bland, Franklin, Wilson, and others. Significantly, as has already been noted, many Tories, such as Galloway, Seabury, and Randolph, recognized the inevitability of some degree of colonial autonomy and even of colonial federation. Thus, on the American side, the whole history of the colonial period reached its climax in the actions of the state conventions and the Continental Congress in the years 1774 and 1775, in the course of which the American Whigs still protested, again and again, their loyalty to the ideals of the British nation and to its symbol, the British King.

It appears, thus, that both English policy and American evolution, during 169 years, had been moving steadily and inevitably toward a political and institutional revision of the imperial constitution that would effectuate an adaptation to these facts. Such a revision, however, did not necessarily mean a dissolution of old, established loyalties.

From the viewpoint of the American Whigs, the accommodation could be made without disturbing old loyalties; on the contrary, the successful transformation could only redound to the greater intensity of the loyalty of the Americans to the British nation and a glorification of its wisdom. For some of the Tories, such a revision was possible; for others, it was not. But for all the Tories, if it ever came to a choice between constitutional revision and their imperial (national) loyalty, the revision must be sacrificed to the higher national values. The break, when it came,

[113]

derived from the determination of the Whigs that they must have the revision; if within the framework of imperial loyalty, well and good; if not, then outside it. For them, their own deepest convictions centered about their sense of need for self-government and the values they identified with that.

This was not yet, in 1776, American nationalism. It was expediency versus loyalty, or British nationalistic idealism. The Tories were idealists; the Whigs were realists.

The Declaration of Independence did not create an American nation, even in the minds of its signers. Nor was a nation created, strictly speaking, during the war years between 1776 and 1783. The Declaration of Independence was an act of secession from the British Empire which incidentally (in the last paragraph) recognized the fact that the "United Colonies," now "Free and Independent States," were joined together in a common cause against Great Britain. It formally severed the ties of loyalty to the Empire to which Burke, Randolph, Dickinson, and Galloway had appealed, but it set up no focal point for a new loyalty, other than the reality of this common cause. Indeed, it seems clear that, for most men, the focal point of one's supreme loyalty was the "Free and Independent State" of which he was a citizen. Men had long been accustomed to speak of "my country" as Virginia or Massachusetts or South Carolina; long before the Revolution this provincial, or colonial, patriotism had moved men without in any way conflicting with their common loyalty to their king as the sovereign symbol of the whole British nation. In the absence of any quickly available, new national concept to take the place of Burke's "empire," and in the presence of the visible states upon which, as colonies, they had for so long fixed their local patriotic feeling, it was probably entirely natural that this state patriotism should have become the dominant loyalty in the new situation and that it should have stood so strongly across the path toward the realization of any national concept.

It was Thomas Burke of North Carolina who was the leading

exponent of the states-sovereignty-states-loyalty school. He embodied his thinking and feeling in the resolution that he introduced into the debate in the Continental Congress on the proposed Articles of Confederation in April 1777 to the effect, as he reported it, that "All sovereign power was in the States separately, and that particular acts of it [the "General Council" of the Confederation], which should be expressly enumerated, would be exercised in conjunction, and not otherwise; but that in all things else each State would exercise all the rights and power of sovereignty, uncontrolled."[38] Burke was surprised and pleased to see that his resolution, adopted as the second article, had such a preponderant weight of support in the Continental Congress:[39] "I was much pleased to find the accumulating powers to Congress so little supported, and I promise myself, in the whole business I shall find my ideas relative thereto nearly similar to those of most of the States. . . . The inequality of the States, and yet the necessity of maintaining their separate independence, will occasion dilemmas almost inextricable."[40] This state loyalty was illustrated by the sort of loyalty oaths the states exacted from their citizens. The following oath, for example, was prescribed by the North Carolina Treason Act of 1777:

> I will bear faithful and true allegiance to the State of North Carolina, and will truly endeavor to support, maintain and defend the independent government thereof, against George the Third of Great Britain, and the attempts of any other Person, Prince, Power or State or Potentate, who by secret acts, Treasons, Compromises, or by open Force shall attempt to subvert the same . . . and that I will disclose and make known to the Governor . . . [or some other officer] all treasons, conspiracies, or attempts committed or intended against the State which shall come to my knowledge.[41]

[38] Thomas Burke to Richard Caswell (governor of North Carolina), Philadelphia, Apr. 29, 1777, in *Letters of Members of the Continental Congress*, ed. E. C. Burnett (8 vols., Washington, D.C., 1921–36), II, 345–46.

[39] The vote was eleven states to one (Virginia) with one state (New Hampshire) divided. (*Ibid.*, 346.)

[40] *Ibid.*

[41] *State Records of North Carolina*, XXIV, II, quoted in Robert O. De-Mond, *The Loyalists in North Carolina during the Revolution* (Durham,

The dominance of the state loyalty sentiment in the thinking and the actions of American leaders was recognized by practically all of them. In the summer of 1776 Edward Rutledge wrote to Robert R. Livingston, "We have done nothing with the confederation for some Days, and it is of little consequence if we never see it again; for we have made such a Devil of it already that the Colonies can never agree to it...."[42] Similar distress over state particularisms was expressed by Samuel Chase, R. H. Lee, and others.[43] Indeed, many American leaders despaired of ever getting the states to confederate, even for the purposes of promoting "the Cause." Conrad-Alexandre Gérard, French minister to the United States, in April 1779 reported Samuel Adams, himself no burning nationalist, as saying that "on voyait de plus en plus qu'il faudroit que les deux empires se separassent, en parlant de ceux de l'Est et du Sud."[44]

The Continental Congress itself carefully recognized state particularisms, presumably based upon state loyalties, in its appeals to the states and their peoples for support of the common cause:

> It is to obtain these things that we call for your strenuous, unremitted exertions. Yet do not believe that you have been, or can be saved merely by your own strength. No! it is by the assistance of Heaven, and this you must assiduously cultivate, by acts which Heaven approves. Thus shall the power and the happiness of these sovereign, free and independent states, founded on the virtue of their citizens, increase, extend and endure, until the Almighty shall blot out all the empires of the earth.[45]

N.C., 1940), 155; see also Harold Hyman, *To Try Men's Souls: Loyalty Tests in American History* (Berkeley, Calif., 1959), facsimile reproductions after p. 208.

[42] *Letters*, ed. Burnett, II, 56.

[43] *Ibid.*, 32 *et passim*.

[44] Conrad-Alexandre Gérard to Comte de Vergennes, Apr. 4, 1779, in *Histoire de la Participation de la France à l'Établissement des États-Unis d'Amérique; Correspondance Diplomatique et Documents*, ed. Henri Doniol (6 vols., Paris, 1890), IV, 106. Gérard, for his own part, later reported "que la paix pourrait se conclure en Europe avant que le Congrès fut d'accord avec lui-même sur la nature des conditions qui doivent y entrer." (*Ibid.*, 223.)

[45] *Journals of the Continental Congress*, ed. Ford *et al.*, XI, 481.

The one thing to which all Americans on the side of independence could, indeed, direct a fervent loyalty was "the Cause."[46] Even Thomas Burke complained against the "jealousies" of the states as injurious to "our common cause."[47]

It was "the Cause," apparently, rather than any clearly ascertainable national ideal, for which Thomas Paine was propagandizing in the early numbers of *The Crisis*. He certainly saw clearly, and used, the concept of a nation in his criticisms of Great Britain:

> There is such an idea existing in the world, as that of *national honor*, and this, falsely understood, is oftentimes the cause of war. ... It is, I think, exceedingly easy to define what ought to be understood by national honor; for that which is the best character for an individual is the best character for a nation; and whenever the latter exceeds or falls beneath the former, there is a departure from the line of true greatness.

> I have thrown out this observation with a design of applying it to Great Britain.... Her idea of national honor seems to consist in national insult, and that to be a great people, is to be neither a Christian, a philosopher, or a gentleman, but to threaten with the rudeness of a bear, and to devour with the ferocity of a lion.[48]

Obviously, Paine's concept of a nation—in this case, the British nation—is crystal clear. Yet he did not quite arrive at the same clarity of national integrity with regard to the United States. His chief concern was for "the Cause": "All we want to know in America is simply this, who is for independence, and who is not?"[49] As yet he was apparently a fervent devotee of "the Cause";

---

[46] Fervor and emotional intensity in support of a common cause must not be confused with nationalism. Many nations may unite in a common cause, and the citizens of all of them support the cause with great intensity, as in the case of the alliance of England, France, Russia, and the United States in the World War of 1914–1918, without feeling a common nationalism. This apparently, was the situation in the United States in the years 1776–1783.

[47] Thomas Burke to Richard Caswell, Apr. 29, 1777, in *Letters*, ed. Burnett, II, 345.

[48] Thomas Paine, *The Crisis* in *The Life and Works of Thomas Paine*, ed. William M. Van der Weyde (3 vols., New Rochelle, N.Y., 1925), III, 77–79.

[49] *Ibid.*, II, 342.

[117]

he had not yet achieved the mental image of the nation that characterized the last few numbers of *The Crisis*.

V

Meanwhile, the march of events of the Revolution was inexorably pushing the Americans toward the formation of an image of a nation, just as the events of 1763-1776 had pushed the Whig-led colonies out of the British Empire.

First of all, the common cause against a common foe drew men together. The mingling of New Englanders, southerners, and Middle State men in the fight against the common enemy must have tended to dull the sharpness of the state loyalty distinctions among them. The adoption of the Articles of Confederation, albeit at first hardly more than a military alliance, did have the effect of organizing the states and their peoples into a viable common institution. Further, the exigencies of the relations of the Confederation with foreign powers forced upon its members a consciousness of the necessity for solidarity in foreign affairs. The alliance with France and the physical presence of French armies and fleets may be supposed to have inspired a consciousness, not only of the common cause but, also, of a common ideal.

Above all, the debate over the disposition to be made of the West—whether to accept the parceling out of the trans-Allegheny lands among the states or to create a national domain as a sort of common property of all the people of all the states—gave impetus to the sort of thinking that must of necessity assume that there was a collective entity composed of all the people of all the states, which, for lack of a better word, many contemporary writers called an "American empire," again echoing the preindependence language and imagery of Edmund Burke.[50]

---

[50] See Paul C. Phillips, "American Opinion Regarding the West, 1778-1783," *Proceedings of the Mississippi Valley Historical Association for the Year 1913-1914* (Cedar Rapids, Iowa, 1914), 286-305.

Nationalism in the American Revolution

The ratification of the Articles of Confederation in 1781 was celebrated editorially by Philadelphia newspapers in terms that go beyond the mere recognition of the successful creation of an effective, practical institution. The *Pennsylvania Packet* remarked on March 3, 1781, that "Thus America, like a well constructed arch, whose parts, harmonizing and mutually supporting each other, all the more closely united the greater the pressure upon them, is growing up in war into greatness and consequence among the nations."[51] On March 7 the *Pennsylvania Gazette* echoed the same sentiment, in almost the same words: "A Union, begun by necessity, cemented by oppression and common danger, and now finally consolidated into a perpetual confederacy of these new and rising states: and thus the United States of America . . . are growing up into conscquence among the nations. . . ."[52] Indeed, the progress of American thinking toward the achievement of a national image is to be seen in the writings of many leaders such as Hamilton, Wilson, Washington, Pelatiah Webster, Madison, and others.

At the same time, too, that the practical exigencies in the course of events were driving men toward a conceptualization of an American nation, intellectuals and publishers were both discovering and creating an American mythos, at both the state and the continental level. Poets, publicists, and politicians exalted the first pioneers who crossed the ocean, American heroes, especially figures who had appeared in the Seven Years' War, American military exploits, the American landscape, American manifest destiny, the epic struggle with the Indians, and so on. It is probably no accident that at least ten American-written narratives of Indian wars and captivities were published in the colonies and states between 1764 and 1780, some of them several times; in addition to which, books like Jeremiah Dummer's *Defence of the New England Charters,* John Wise's *Vindication of the Governments*

---

[51] Quoted in *Letters,* ed. Burnett, VI, 1-2, n. 2.
[52] *Ibid.*

of the New England Churches, and Mayhew's sermon on *Unlimited Submission* were printed in new editions. Again and again, also, reference was made, by both Whig and Tory writers, to the English mythos of liberty inherited by Americans and to the fact that British blood still flowed in American veins. As the war progressed, the heroic deeds and men of that struggle became part of the American mythos. Freneau, for example, conceived a bitter hatred for Britain and all its works and in poem after poem celebrated and promoted the heroic actions of "the Cause." Freneau's bitternes and belligerency are shown by such poems as "A Political Litany," "American Liberty," and "The British Prison Ship." And he made substantial contributions to the growth of an American mythos with such poems as "On the Memorable Victory of Paul Jones," "To the Memory of the Brave Americans," and others.[53]

Americans were becoming conscious of their own heroic past and their own culture, as well as of the English traditions that they had inherited. The birth of an American mythos, and of the consciousness of a native American culture, was one of the incidents in the progress of Americans toward a full national consciousness—a growing self-consciousness which began to demand cultural as well as political independence from Great Britain.

VI

Many forces were at work, then, to create an American national image, to disseminate it among the people of the states, and gradually to arouse a universal loyalty to it. Some American leaders caught the vision, as it were, gradually, and, by the end of the war, were recognizable American nationalists.

The most famous outburst of this sentiment, of course, was Patrick Henry's impulsive exclamation to the Continental Con-

[53] *Poems of Philip Freneau,* ed. Pattee, I, 139-41, 162; II, 18-39, 75-80, 101-102.

gress in 1774 that "The distinctions between Virginians, Pennsylvanians, New Yorkers, and New Englanders, are no more. I am not a Virginian, but an American."[54] But there were others.

One such was that of Peter Thatcher of Watertown, Massachusetts, who delivered an impassioned oration on March 5, 1776, four months before the Declaration of Independence: "The tender feelings of the human heart are deeply affected with the fate of [General Richard Montgomery] and the other heroes who have bled and died, that their country may be free; but at the same time, sensations of indignant wrath are excited in the breasts of every friend of freedom. . . ."[55] Here was loyalty to a cause, but it was also an appeal to the loyalty of his hearers to "the rising empire of America":

> Let us then arouse to arms; for, upon our exertions depends [our descendants'] freedom; upon our exertions depends the important question, whether the rising empire of America, shall be an empire of slaves or of freemen.

> Animated by these considerations, my friends and fellow-citizens, let us strain every nerve in the service of our country! what are our lives when viewed in competition with the happiness of such an empire! what is our private interest when opposed to that of three millions of men! let our bosoms glow with the warmth of patriotism; let us sacrifice our ease, our fortunes, and our lives, that we may save our country. . . .[56]

In the *Continentalist,* Hamilton argued for a "continental" concept of the United States, and in language that has a clearly national flavor. And he concluded, "Happy America, if those to whom thou hast intrusted the guardianship of thy infancy know how to provide for the future repose, but miserable and undone, if their negligence or ignorance permits the spirit of discord to

[54] Robert Douthat Meade, *Patrick Henry, Patriot in the Making* (Philadelphia, 1957), 325.

[55] "Oration delivered at Watertown [Mass.], March 5, 1776, by Peter Thatcher, M.A.," in *Principles and Acts of the Revolution in America,* ed. Niles, 45.

[56] *Ibid.,* 46.

crest her banner on the ruins of thy tranquility."[57] It cannot be said unequivocally that Hamilton was motivated, in his writings during the war years, by loyalty to a national ideal as against the promptings of his supreme genius for the expedient and the practical—for a constitution that would work. The same uncertainty applies to Pelatiah Webster, who published a proposal for a strong central government just at the end of the war, in 1783.[58] Webster's thinking was concerned with the philosophy of the state, rather than with any image of a nation: "A number of sovereign States united into one Commonwealth, and appointing a supreme power to manage the affairs of the union, *do necessarily and unavoidably part with and transfer over to such supreme power, so much of their own sovereignty, as is necessary to render the ends of the union effectual....* Just so, every member of civil society parts with many of his natural rights, that he may enjoy the rest in greater security under the protection of society."[59] Here is no question of emotional loyalty; the image is that of a body politic formed under the terms of a social compact, not clearly, however, one of a nation.

With Dr. David Ramsay of South Carolina, however, the concept of an American nation seems clear; the sentiment expressed seems obviously to be an American nationalism. In what may have been the first Fourth of July oration in American history, on the second anniversary of the Declaration of Independence (1778), Ramsay glorified the qualities and the destiny of the United States in terms that are unmistakably nationalistic:

> I appeal, to the experience of all, whether they do not feel an elevation of soul growing out of the emancipation of their country....
>
> We have laid the foundations of a new empire, which promises to

[57] *Works of Alexander Hamilton,* ed. Lodge, I, 287.
[58] Pelatiah Webster, *A Dissertation on the Political Union and Constitution of the Thirteen United States of North-America; Which is Necessary to Their Preservation and Happiness* (Hartford, Conn., 1783).
[59] *Ibid.,* 3.

enlarge itself into vast dimensions, and to give happiness to a great continent. It is now our turn to figure on the face of the earth, and in the annals of the world. . . .

Ever since the flood, true religion, arts, empire, and riches, have taken a slow and gradual course from east to west, and are now about fixing their long and favourite abode in this new western world. . . . Our Independence will redeem one quarter of the globe from tyranny and oppression, and consecrate it the chosen seat of truth, justice, freedom, and religion. . . . Generations yet unborn will bless us for the blood-bought inheritance, we are about to bequeath them. Oh happy times! Oh glorious days! Oh kind, indulgent, bountiful Providence, that we live in this favoured period, and have the honour of helping forward these great events, and of suffering in a cause of such infinite importance![60]

In the last numbers of *The Crisis*, Paine approached such a concept rather more closely and clearly than either Hamilton or Webster. And in his valedictory,[61] the concept of the American nation became clear and explicit:

But that which must more forcibly strike a thoughtful, penetrating mind, and which includes and renders all inferior concerns, is the Union of the States. On this our great national character depends. . . . It is through this only that we are, or can be, nationally known in the world; it is the flag of the United States which renders our ships and commerce safe on the seas, or in a foreign port. . . .

The division of the empire into states is for our own convenience, but abroad this distinction ceases. . . . In short, we have no other national sovereignty than as United States. . . .

Our citizenship in the United States is our national character. Our citizenship in any particular state is only our local distinction. . . . Our great title is Americans—our inferior one varies with the place.[62]

The development of Paine's thought and feeling, traced through his writings from the period in 1775 when he was writing

[60] *United States Magazine*, I (Jan., Mar. 1779), 24, 106.
[61] *The Crisis*, No. 13, 1783, in *Life and Works of Thomas Paine*, ed. Van der Weyde, III, 77-79.
[62] *Ibid.*, 243-45.

for the *Pennsylvania Magazine,* through *The Crisis* essays, shows a clear progression from the position of an English nationalist to that of an American nationalist. The metamorphosis was not sudden or abrupt, but it did take place. In this fact, Paine was probably typical of many, if not most, Americans.

VII

Among the poets, the preachers, and the publicists—the men of fancy and creative imagination—the image of an American nation may have emerged more early and more clearly than in the minds and hearts of the politicians. In the poems of Freneau, the outstanding poet of the Revolution, the reorientation of emotional direction closely parallels that which took place in the writings of Paine. Thus, whereas, even as late as 1775, Freneau dreamed of a reformed Britain and a restored British national felicity, by 1778 he was also discovering in his poetry a concept of an American "empire," or nation, composed of all the people of the thirteen states:

> America! The works of peace be thine,
> Thus shalt thou gain a triumph more divine—
> To thee belongs a second golden reign,
> Thine is the empire o'er a peaceful main;
> Protect the rights of human kind below,
> Crush the proud tyrant who becomes their foe,
> And future times shall own your struggles blest,
> And future years enjoy perpetual rest.
> ....
> A glorious empire rises, bright and new!
> Firm be the structure, and must rest on you!—[63]

Freneau continued to glorify the separate states, however, and although in his address to Washington's officers (1781) he called upon them to

[63] *Poems of Philip Freneau,* ed. Pattee, I, 281-82.

> Accept, great men, that share of honest praise
> A grateful nation to your merit pays:

he continued, reviewing the conflict just ended,

> Resist! resist! was heard through every state,
> You heard the call, and feared your country's fate;[64]

leaving some ambiguity as to whether he was thinking of a genuine American nation or an alliance, whether he was celebrating the triumph of a nation or that of a cause. In the light of his later Jeffersonian politics, it might be doubted whether he was ever wholly a nationalist in the supreme sense of the word.

Among other poets, Timothy Dwight and Joel Barlow showed a similar progression of thought toward the concept of an American nation. In his poem "Columbia," Dwight may have come closer to achieving the concept than even Freneau:

> Columbia, Columbia, to glory arise,
> The queen of the world, and the child of the skies!
> Thy genius commands thee; with rapture behold,
> While ages on ages thy splendors unfold.
>
> ....
>
> A world is thy realm: for a world be thy laws,
> Enlarg'd as thine empire, and just as thy cause;
> On freedom's broad basis, that empire shall rise,
> Extend with the main, and dissolve with the skies.[65]

Joel Barlow's "The Vision of Columbus," begun while he was a student at Yale, also caught the vision of an American nation and contributed to the creation of an American mythos:

---

[64] *Ibid.,* II, 81-83.

[65] Timothy Dwight, "Columbia," in *The Connecticut Wits,* ed. Vernon L. Parrington (New York, 1926), 273-74. Use of the term "Columbia" to designate the *ensemble* of the thirteen seceded states was customary among the writers of the war years. Freneau, for example, used it frequently. In a footnote to his poem "American Liberty" (1775) Freneau explained the term thus: "Columbia, America sometimes so-called from Columbus, the first discoverer." *(Poems of Philip Freneau,* ed. Pattee, I, 142.) He also used, in a similar sense, the term "New Albion." In another footnote to "American Liberty" he explained this term thus: "New Albion, properly New England, but is often applied to all British America." *(Ibid.,* 145).

Each orient realm, the former pride of earth,
Where men and science drew their ancient birth,
Shall soon behold, on this enlighten'd coast,
Their fame transcended and their glory lost.[66]

H. H. Brackenridge showed a similar progression of thought. After a series of poems on "the Cause," the most notable of which are "Bunker Hill" (1776) and "The Death of General Montgomery" (1777), he went on to become editor of the *United States Magazine,* which he made a vehicle for American cultural independence. He published the text of David Ramsay's "Oration, on the Anniversary of Independence," and editorialized upon it in a vein that betrays his nationalism for a "United [American] Empire":

> In America we see a fair establishment of equal liberty and a new stage erected for every display of immortal and divine eloquence in honor of those who had offered up their lives in defence of their country; or of those who by the invention or improvement of useful arts have done good to mankind; or in celebration of the anniversary of some great event, such as the declaration of independence of this United Empire.[67]

It seems evident, then, that the concept of an "American empire," or nation, which replaced the image of the British imperial society to which men had given their loyalty before 1775 in their minds and hearts, was the product of a slow intellectual and emotional growth. It began, perhaps, in the sort of patriotism toward the provinces expressed by colonial writers or, it may be, in the devotion to "America" felt by Galloway. But it was many years before the image of the British empire-nation of the colonial era was fully and perfectly replaced in the minds of all Americans by the image of a genuine, integral American nation. The war years, 1776-1783, constituted what might be called the period of its gestation and, toward the end of the war, its birth.

[66] Joel Barlow, *The Vision of Columbus* (Hartford, Conn., 1787), 189.
[67] "Remarks on Ramsay's Oration, on the Anniversary of Independence," *United States Magazine,* I (Jan. 1779), 21; the text of Ramsay's oration is printed on pages 20-22.

PART III

Philosophy of History

THE FLIGHT FROM REASON

IN A recent article[1] Reinhold Niebuhr has this to say about our historical moment: "The civilization that we are now defending against the attack of a synthetic barbarism .... finds itself in one of the deepest crises of world history in our own generation" (p. 100). The nature of the crisis, he says, is that of "a breakdown both in the organization of civilization and in the life of a culture." It is "a spiritual as well as a political and economic crisis" (p. 131). The solution for the crisis he finds to be a return to the Christian faith.

Niebuhr is only one of many men of our time who are reacting against the belief in the primacy of reason in human conduct and human history. Disappointed by the apparent failure of eighteenth- and nineteenth-century rationalism based on science, disillusioned with the optimism of Herbert Spencer, and distressed by the seeming "spiritual emptiness" of the age of materialism, they have sought to recover a condition of society, real or imagined, in which the emotional, or spiritual, side of man would be given greater recognition and opportunity for expression. Their writings take the form of a protest against the shortcomings

[1] "A Faith for History's Greatest Crisis," *Fortune,* XXVI (1942), 99-100, 122, 125, 126, 128, and 131.

[129]

of rationalism or attempt, as Gerald Heard put it in 1931, to show that "Winwood Read and Herbert Spencer can be reconciled."[2] The work of Vilfredo Pareto was a significant and provocative attempt—to say the least—to demonstrate that men act first on the basis of sentiments ("residues") and think afterward ("derivatives") to explain their actions. Oswald Spengler, seeing in the present stage of Western civilization a moment of decline, attributed that decline,[3] which he called a "morphological" one, to a natural and inevitable organic process in history that men are powerless, by the exercise of their own reason, either to cause or to prevent. Arnold Toynbee, seeking the cause of the decline of civilizations, apparently finds it in what he calls the "schism of the soul,"[4] which is essentially a conflict between the long-term intelligence, or reason, in a society and the nonrational, selfish, short-term impulses and desires of its members.

The two books[5] to be discussed here start with similar presumptions of the imminence of civilization's collapse and the inadequacy of reason to meet it. But one of them (Mumford's), as distinguished from the works of Niebuhr or Spengler, insists that man, by taking thought of his personality, the most important part of which is its nonrational part, can, by his own power, improve his condition and save his civilization from the abyss. The other (Kahler's), while admitting a certain influence of reason, would have us believe that the course of human evolution will carry us past the crisis safely, almost regardless of what we do. Both, in other words, believe civilization is in the midst of a great crisis, threatening catastrophe; both place great emphasis upon the nonrational elements in human nature as indices of human conduct and as determinants of human history.

[2] Gerald HEARD, *Emergence of Man* (London, 1931), p. 13.
[3] *Decline of the West* (New York, 1939), especially chapters i, iii, and iv.
[4] *Study of History* (6 vols.; London, 1935-39), especially Vol. V.
[5] Erich KAHLER. *Man the Measure*. New York: Pantheon Books, Inc., 1944. Pp. 671. $5.00. Lewis MUMFORD. *Condition of Man*. New York: Harcourt, Brace & Co., 1944. Pp. 447. $5.00.

The Flight from Reason

Now there appears to be in the findings of modern psychology a certain amount of scientific justification for this general position with regard to human nature. The psychologists seem to be far from agreed among themselves as to the nature and the operation of the human mind. For at one extreme stand the behaviorists, followers of John B. Watson, who dismiss altogether the concept of consciousness and, having dismissed all the dualistic psychological systems built upon the two concepts of "mind" and "matter," base their whole monistic explanation of human behavior upon the observable "conditioned reflexes" of a purely material or animal organism known as "man." At the other extreme stand the psychoanalysts, followers of Sigmund Freud, who today believe that the psychic life of the individual takes place on three levels—the *id,* the *ego,* and the *superego*—the id being the subconscious animal inheritance of instincts and impulses, the ego being the conscious self, and the superego being, not merely a sort of conscience, but also a positive, creative, and directive agency with a vague sort of authority over the whole.

Between these two extremes there are many other schools of thought, giving a varying emphasis to the rational or conscious, as opposed to the nonrational or subconscious, elements of the human mind. Thus the psychologists have many different interpretations of human behavior. They are all approximately agreed, however, on two things: first, the fact that man is not essentially different from the other animals, and, second, that the "rational" element in human behavior is of considerably less importance than formerly supposed and may be much less important than the primitive, animal, and irrational impulses. In other words, the conduct of man himself is less "rational" than "animal" or "irrational." Thus, if there is any mental characteristic of man that distinguishes him from other animals, it is the degree of development of his mind rather than any single aspect of it. On this general position most modern psychologists seem to be substantially agreed.

Now the historian of the present and the future must, doubtless, take into account the findings of psychology, the science of human behavior. For the historian is not merely a narrator of human events; he is also their explainer. And even though the findings of psychology are as yet unstandardized, controversial, and fairly undependable, it is difficult to imagine, for example, a satisfactory history of the "age of Adolf Hitler" being written by any historian lacking a workable concept of the operation of the human mind, both in the individual and in the social group. But the historian who accepts behaviorism as the explanation of human action will write one sort of history; the historian who accepts the findings of the functional school of psychology will write another; the believer in Gestalt psychology another; the Freudian another; and so on. It does seem safe now, nevertheless, for the historian to accept the findings upon which most of the psychologists agree—such, for example, as the relative importance of the primitive, irrational elements in human nature and the relative unimportance of the rational. This, alone, may probably have a considerable effect upon the writing of history, as also, probably, may the concept of the normal individual as a monistic entity, without any distinction between "body" and "soul" or between "reason" and "nonreason." While the facts of history do not seem, in any single instance, to justify the application of this concept of the monistic individual to a society or a civilization as a whole, yet this concept does suggest a certain plausibility for what Spengler calls the "morphology" of a civilization—that is to say, the organic unity of all its aspects taken together. The effect of this idea upon the writing of history has been the many efforts to present the history of civilization as one seamless whole and the conviction in the minds of an increasing number of historians that history presented in any other way can only result in a partial or a distorted account. The school of psychology—if, indeed, it can be called a school at all—that appears most substantially to give scientific support to such an approach to the human record is the so-called "dynamic school" at Columbia University, of which the outstanding leader has been Robert Woodworth, for this school is essentially monistic in its general attitude toward the human mind. While it recognizes behavior in which the rational element is not present, it rejects any dualistic division into conscious mind and unconscious mind, or anything of the sort, and thinks of the whole mind as essentially one and of conscious intelligence as the guiding directive element.

In other words, despite the difference between schools of psychology, there appears, from their common findings, to be a certain amount of scientific justification for two trends that have recently appeared in certain historical writings. The first of these is the effort to present the history of man in its entirety, more or less with the purpose of understanding man himself by a study of his history. The second is the tendency to place a much greater emphasis than formerly upon the irrational elements in human behavior. A third tendency—to see in the present historical moment a deep, even catastrophic crisis that threatens to carry our civilization to its ruin—is widespread but apparently cannot call to its support any such formidable array of scientific data as the first two can. All three of these tendencies are to be observed in many of the historical and sociological works now being written. Two of the books that illustrate these three trends are those to be discussed here.

These two books are not to be regarded primarily as history but rather as studies of man, particularly of man as he is right now. For Mumford, history is used merely to explain the present; for Kahler, history is the record of human evolution, in a certain critical stage in which we now find ourselves. Both find mankind at present in the midst of a fearful crisis threatening an unspoken doom; both prescribe remedies—although Kahler thinks the remedy will force itself upon us in the normal continuance of the evolutionary process. Both, too, are psychologists in the sense

[133]

that they rest their explanation of the course of human history upon what they understand to be the peculiar characteristics of the human mind or spirit. To Mumford it appears:

> The period through which we are living presents itself as one of unmitigated confusion and disintegration.... But behind all these phenomena of physical destruction we can detect an earlier and perhaps more fundamental series of changes: a loss of communion between classes and peoples, a breakdown in stable behaviour, a loss of form and purpose in many of the arts, with a growing emphasis on the accidental and the trivial: in short, the earliest form of this crisis was an internal "schism of the soul," as Toynbee calls it, and a break up of the over-all pattern of meaning [p. 14].

Mumford is frankly and completely Freudian in his interpretation of human nature—except that he improves upon Freud by considering the superego as a positive, creative element rather than the negative, disciplinary agency that Freud thought it to be. And he adopts the psychoanalytic method for civilization: "People whose course of life has reached a crisis must confront their collective past as fully as a neurotic patient must unbury his personal life: long-forgotten traumas in history may have a disastrous effect upon millions who remain unaware of them" *(ibid)*. Having set himself the task of psychoanalyzing modern civilization, Mumford proceeds to write his history like the psychoanalyst reviewing the case of his patient. It would be impossible here to follow in detail this process of psychoanalyzing an entire civilization, but a few sample expressions of Mumford's psychoanalysis may be given. For example, with regard to the Hellenistic age he says: "Frustration and a sense of guilt appeared in Hellenic culture in the second half of the fifth century. And one fact makes it plain that this guilt was almost universally shared: a religious cult, or a series of them, came into existence and attempted to lift the heavy burden, bringing the excluded classes and the rejected impulses back into the circle of the human" (pp. 25-26). Concerning the Romanesque age he writes: "There is scarcely a single aspect of this culture which does not become clearer when one interprets it as a neurotic dream phenomenon" (p. 107). On the Middle Ages, he says: "The Catholic Church had no mold for the life that Abelard and Héloise were capable of living and sharing: it had opened too wide a gap between the erotic and the spiritual; and though it could by a rigorous sublimation give to the latter some of the benefit of its erotic energy, it had no formula for the reverse process" (p. 116). And: "Medieval Christianity, in the act of holding the superego at an impossible height, had helped to create this dualism, this ambivalence, this intolerable tension" (p. 158). He writes regarding the modern age: "But although mammonism and mechanism were the two great molders of human character between the sixteenth and the twentieth centuries, they were attached to a negative super-ego, that which had been created by the Christian Church ... the dissolution of the medieval synthesis had given rise to a counter-movement: an uprush of the libido, an intensification of the senses, an introduction of the mind to its own labyrinths, an expansion of every activity that promoted animation, joy, bodily exuberance" (p. 201). And: "Do not underestimate the contribution of the painter [in the baroque age]: He remodeled the sexual superego" (p. 211).

But Mumford's history, as history, is full of astonishing statements of fact and interpretations. Some of these are of such an arresting nature as to invite a really serious attention by trained historians. Only a few can be given here. With regard to Protestantism he takes issue with the prevailing point of view:

> Protestantism in religion came into being, not as an ally of capitalism, but as its chief enemy: not as an effort to swell the energies of the *id* but to curb them before they became too powerful. This fact has been too lightly passed over by those too innocent historians who date the rise of Protestantism from the sixteenth century..... Instead of Protestantism's being the new creed of the rising bourgeoisie, Protestantism when it appeared in the twelfth century was an attempt to prevent the rise of the bourgeoisie. For the most stubborn challenge to the Roman Church came from those

who were sickened by the spectacle of its open alliance with capitalism: it came from those who wished to do away with the venal
elements that were making a mockery of its sacred professions
[p. 182].

Regarding the age of explorations, he asks:

What were exploring and pioneering and colonization but an
attempt to consign the past itself to the lumber-room, and to solve
man's social problems, not by disciplining and refining his whole
nature but by changing his background alone? [p. 238].

The baroque age receives a quite unorthodox explanation:

The most revolutionary invention of modern times [contracep-
tion], even more significant to humanity than the printing press,
made headway, not as a beneficent aid to family life, not as a contribution to erotic culture, but as a safeguard against disease and a
device for making possible an irresponsible sterility.

[In a strongly libidinous age] the effect of a more copious demand for sexual enjoyment would be felt within [faithful] mar-
riages: in seeking to meet outside competition the loyal wife might
attempt to fill a sexual demand that a less voluptuous age would
hardly be conscious of: similarly the wider provenance of sexual
images and symbols would deepen the unconscious suggestions of
sex. This happened in the baroque period: witness not merely
the decorative use of the spiral and the scalloped shell and the
cornucopia, but even the one fresh element in building, the staircase. The formal staircase may have been in origin what it now is
in dream—a symbol of the sexual act, projected into space and
formally embodied in the setting of the palace; for the grand stairs
led from the public rooms on the lower stories, where the charms of
sex were exhibited, to the bedrooms in the upper stories where they
were fulfilled [p. 214].

No serious historian can accept statements such as the ones
about contraception and the staircase, since they are undocumented. The statement with regard to colonization, furthermore,
is not merely undocumented; it exemplifies the central and most
fundamental fault of the book. In speaking of the exploring
and colonization of the age of overseas expansion as an attempt
to consign the past to the lumber-room and to solve man's social
problems by evading self-discipline and changing the scene,
Mumford flies in the face of the obvious facts. For assuming

that the actions of the explorers and colonizers were rationally self-directed—that is, that they knew what they were doing—it is crystal clear, by a study of the documents, that the vast majority of those men entered into that great event for the sake of making money. Some there were, indeed—a small fraction—in whose minds one of the many motives present was the desire to escape religious persecution. Others there were, also, who became explorers because of their intellectual or scientific curiosity. Still others felt, along with other motives, a rising nationalistic urge to outdo their national enemies. There were a few Englishmen, to be sure, who at one moment thought of their native land as overpopulated and of the colonies as an outlet for surplus population; and there were others who saw in the colonies an outlet for criminals and social misfits. But those who thought in terms of overpopulation quickly changed their minds, and the use of colonies as a dumping ground for criminals never had any long-term significance, with the exception of one case (Australia); and even that one offers convincing evidence that rational self-direction is a more important determinant of history than the libido.

Only by a forced and completely undocumented conviction that those men and women who produced the age of expansion were driven by motives of which they were completely unconscious can one force one's self to believe that they were attempting to do anything at all with regard to the past or that, with the exceptions noted, they were even conscious that there were any social problems involved. Their eyes were almost exclusively fixed upon the future; and, far from presenting any social problems, that future was so bright and so exciting as to offer almost anything imaginable to any man. Their feeling was a positive expansive feeling; most of them were not motivated by a desire to solve social problems, or even of escape. No more than (though just as much as) the frontiersman who feels that there is better land farther on and moves out to it is motivated by a desire to solve social problems and to escape from the proximity of his neighbors.

Thus a fundamental and completely devastating criticism of Mumford as a historian arises from his determination to force into the narrative of history an interpretation of human behavior that has no more than the slightest conceivable justification in the documentary evidence. No trained historian, therefore, can accept either Mumford's statements of fact or his interpretations, in which every fact is forced into a preconceived explanation of human behavior—especially since his Freudian explanation still falls far short of convincing scientific psychologists of either its adequacy or its completeness.

But even if Mumford's history were accurate and his interpretation reasonably sound, the historian would have to take him to task for his constant editorializing on the morality of his human subjects. For example, with regard to Machiavelli, he states:

> It is this capacity for both badness and goodness, for conduct that would disgrace a healthy animal and for conduct that would honor an angel, that gives human character its range, its variety, its unexpected debacles and upsurges. Man's very loyalty to symbols, to "mere" words, and "mere" personal feelings, confounds every purely materialistic code of conduct. . . . [Machiavelli's] political philosophy accounted for an Alexander, a Caligula, a Frederick II, a Cesare Borgia; but it had no key to the character of a Demosthenes, a Thomas More, a Garibaldi, or an Abraham Lincoln [p. 173].

Mumford is, above all, a moralist. His editorials on historical events and personalities are moral editorials. He is fervently devoted to the discovery and the dissemination of "values," although he is never very clear as to what those values are. The aim of this book, the third and last in a series of which the first two were *Technics and Civilization* (New York, 1934) and *The Culture of Cities* (New York, 1938), as he says in the preface to this one, "has been to give a rounded interpretation of the development of modern man, and to show what changes in his plan of life are necessary if he is to make the most of the vast powers that are now his to command." These books, he continues, were written during a period of rapid social disintegration. "Not once, but repeatedly in man's history, has an all-enveloping crisis provided the condition essential to a renewal of the personality and the community. In the darkness of the present day, that memory is also a promise." And on page 413 he says: "We must create a new idolum: we must create a new super-ego: we must create a fresh plan of life, and we must educate ourselves and discipline ourselves for quite different tasks than those that commanded us during the period of expansion. In the course of this reorientation the subjective and the objective, the primitive and the cultivated, the mechanical and the human will finally be unified in a new organic whole, which will do justice to the entire nature of man."

Erich Kahler's concept of history is noticeably different from that of Mumford, although his attitude toward the subject—his mood—is quite similar.

For Kahler:

> History implies a continuity of something more than time; only if history can be seen as a one and consistent human evolution, only then has it a meaning..... Eternity has no history, and neither has chaos..... The unity of humanity and the unity of history, stand and fall together; both originate in the Christian world religion..... What we call history begins with the Jewish-Christian concept of man as the image of God, the creator of the universe..... The subject matter of history, however, was not exactly man as a secular entity, but the spiritual welfare of the human soul, the purification of the soul and its approach to God [pp. 4-5].

Now, while Kahler is not an adherent of any particular school of psychology, he does premise his entire explanation of human history upon the peculiarly human quality that distinguishes man from the lower animals. It is only this human quality that makes it possible for man to have a history. And it is only this that gives that history meaning. The importance he attaches to this human spirit is clear when he writes: "The exclusively human feature we are seeking is to be found not in any partial functioning of the human constitution, but rather in a general quality of man that is the pivot of all the various achievements and manifestations of his civilization, a quality that cannot be localized anatomically or physiologically, but that emerges gradually from the complex totality of the human organism. This is *man's faculty of going beyond himself,* of transcending the limits of his own physical being. This quality .... does not coincide with reason, for it manifests itself not only intellectually but emotionally" (p. 11). This is the psychological, or spiritual, quality of human beings, as Kahler conceives it, that distinguishes man from the animals. If history for Mumford is a history of the human psychological condition, for Kohler it is a history of the evolution of this human spirit.

There appears at this point an interesting difference between Mumford and Kahler. Mumford seems hardly conscious of cultures other than that known as Western civilization, although he speaks as though he meant to include all of mankind. Kahler, on the other hand, is conscious of the other great culture-patterns. But he finds the others either at lower levels of evolutionary developments or, as in the case of India, proceeding in a direction the reverse of our own, in that "it leads altogether away from earthly, temporal life . . . [and proceeds toward] motionlessness so absolute that it attains nothingness . . . [as] its most sublime, its most valued, concept" (p. 23). Since Western civilization has gone farthest in the evolution of the dynamics of the human spirit, it may be taken as "the leading and representative trend of human evolution" (p. 24).

Kahler, too, is a moralist: "The whole problem of human progress," he says, "is a moral one, with which we cannot deal until we have done what we can to understand the condition of

[140]

our world through investigating human evolution." He goes on to say, however, that, "although morality and organized welfare form an integral part of human evolution, ... a specifically moral point of view would only serve to blur our subject" (p. 17). Hence, despite his stated purpose to write history as history, he, too, cannot refrain from editorializing. His great devil is economic materialism, the concomitant of capitalism, the origin of which he finds in the German commercial cities of the late Middle Ages and the Renaissance. Describing the emergence of capitalism in these cities, he says:

> Here, for the first time, in this German epoch and in these German cities, business in itself, money-making in itself, production of goods and heaping up of comforts, assumed such power over man that he spent all of his vitality, his heart, all his present and future, all his *human being*, in the literal sense of the word, in a restless, a persistent growing and devouring production per se, a production, the final meaning of which he has completely lost and forgotten. And this was the beginning of capitalism, which is the rule of capital over man, the rule of the economic function over the human heart [p. 313].

Later (pp. 618-19) he discovers the new principle, the saving principle which need not be invented. This new and saving principle is collectivism.

> It emerges from the second, subterranean development that accompanies capitalistic development, the inevitability of which capitalists refuse to see. This second development is inherent in the development of technics .... sheer self-preservation leaves us no alternative but to recognize and act according to the direction of human unity, and this means, to make the latent collective of men into an open collective. The *human collective* toward which the technical interconnection of our world has pointed a brutal way implies the sovereignty of man, of the *welfare of man*, over the rule of things and their production. Being one and organic, involved with human unity and governed by the requirements of man, it is diametrically opposed to the many private collectives, which, governed by the laws of production, must follow the mechanical exactions of objects.

Collectivism, the saving principle, is also, with Kahler, a moral

[141]

principle. And the salvation of civilization will be achieved only by the collective, transcendent, human spirit, which is something quite apart from individual will or individual reason.

> The notion of the identity of self-interest and common interest [he states (pp. 635-37)] must be taken as a start for changing the constitution of the world itself, so that what is necessary may become possible: to live and to act in accordance with a Christian civilization.
>
> Of course, a merely rational appeal to the self-interest of the individual is not enough. Practical self-interest is not the only motive that activates man. He has his irrational individual passions and urges which drive him on, sublimated or not. But there is a still deeper irrational stratum where an innate anxiety, a shudder of loneliness and forsakenness, a sense of homelessness in the universe, a vital need for super-individual support and comfort, are alive. These anxieties and needs are even more deep-rooted than and at least as real and concrete as rational self-interest and individual passions..... In modern man they are mostly left to themselves, they are neglected and half-buried, and many people hardly know any longer that they exist. Yet the more complex modern life becomes, the more difficult to understand, the more this fear amounting to panic, the more this need for super-individual support grows. Left to themselves, these urges find their outlet in the forms of uncontrolled emotion and mass hysteria we have experienced in our time.....
>
> [In all those] whose faith in God has lost its vitality, the human faculty of transcending will go on turning to inhuman ends and leading to disaster until there grows upon them a faith in the idea of man in a pure and unveiled form, a Religio Humana.

Here, at last, is Kahler's doctrine—"the religion of the human." And yet, despite all this moralizing, there seems to be little that man, by his own efforts, can do to better his condition.

> What this book was intended to show [he says] is that history is not an accidental conglomerate of events, not the deliberate accomplishment of individuals, but a connected whole, the unified, consistent development of an organic being that is man. History is a unity, it has a meaning, and so it has a definite direction. This direction is not merely the work of man's will, nor can he alter it by an act of will any more than the phases of youth, maturity and age can be altered within an individual. Man can determine himself, but only in so far as he recognizes the processes of his nature,

as he foresees the tendency of development, smooths its path and exploits its forces.... But even in his most Promethean achievements man with all his insight and foresight has done no more than further an evolution whose germs and scope lay beyond his power [pp. 607-8].

Kahler is never quite clear, however, as to just how much individual men can do to save civilization from its doom. Apparently, the new humanism, the new *religio humana,* is to arise from the collective human mind and soul. Finally, he declares: "The idea of man, the counsel of a new humanism, are certainly the very last things to move the present world to a fundamental change. But we may expect this idea to force itself upon men when the course of events brings them to see that without human community and fraternity they are all lost together, that man needs goodness as he needs his daily bread" (p. 640). Thus the "idea of Man" is urgent and vital; but it will come to us of itself, for in due course it will force itself upon us. Apparently, we are in the midst of the gravest of all human crises, but there seems to be no cause for worry—the normal course of evolution will take care of us.

Kahler's doctrine of the evolution of the human spirit, for all that, has ingenuity and integrity. The human spirit, as he sees it, passed through three stages in its evolution from the brute animal to the modern human: at first, man learned to distinguish himself from his ancestors, his gods; second, he distinguished self from the universe; third, he transcended self in his relationship with the universe and with his fellow-men. Through all these stages the human spirit moves through a greater and greater refinement and achieves a more and more complete transcendence of self. Apparently, in the next stage, the era of the human collective, man will achieve something approximating a complete selflessness—a transcendence of self in the interests of the collective.

The idea has consistency, although it cannot be documented;

and it will provide the historians with much food for thought. But it is more Hegelianism than history. If Mumford, as historian, is a Freudian mystic and romantic, improved, then Kahler, as historian, is an improved Hegelian.

Now the appeal from a purely rationalistic explanation of human behavior, either to the Freudian "organic humanism" of Mumford, on the one hand, or to the *"religio humana"* of Kahler, on the other, is an abandonment of any belief that human reason alone can determine human history. As a reaction against simple eighteenth-century rationalism, this intellectual temper, this mood to admit the nonrational as a factor in human history, on the basis of the findings of psychology, is both legitimate and valid. That the human mind, even in the heroes and makers of history, to say nothing of the unsung and inarticulate masses, often acts upon sheer, irrational, animal impulses, is documented by every page of the record, as well as by the findings of modern psychology. Yet, for the purposes of history writing, it is probably safe to say that if the "drives" underlying human behavior in the past have been fundamentally and predominantly the so-called "animal" drives, nevertheless the development of civilization and the major events of human history have resulted from the conscious direction of those forces by human reason, or intelligence; and that the conflicting interests that produced struggle and conflict, and the thought and aspiration that produced religion, art, music, and philosophy, as well as the drives that produced economic, social, and political institutions, might all be explained, were all the conditions known, in terms of the dynamic psychologist's formula of stimulus→condition of the organism→response.

The acceptance of this fairly conservative "psychology of history" would not, of course, rule out such a thing as sex, for example, as a determinant of human history. For of sex and its influence there is abundant documentation. But the recognition of sex as a historical force does not mean the acceptance, either entirely or exclusively, of the Freudian explanation of human history as Mumford accepts it. On the other hand, since the historian is not a metaphysician, the tentative acceptance of the dynamic brand of psychology also rules out any historical discussion of the human spirit (except as an idea), since the human spirit as a thing cannot be identified and documented historically as an observable part of physical, mental, or social man.

A similar conclusion must be drawn with regard to the consideration of "values." Both of these books start with the assumption that Western civilization is now in the midst of a great and dangerous crisis. Both agree that the crisis is due to the loss of a sense of values. Both conclude that civilization can be saved only by the recovery and the dominance of certain "values." Mumford believes it can be done by conscious effort, while Kahler thinks that the desired values will probably come to dominate human destiny in the course of the future evolution of the human spirit with or without the conscious aid of men. Both place great emphasis upon the nonrational elements in human behavior as sources of the so-called "values." Historically, Mumford is probably correct when he says: "Since value is integral to all human experience, a theory that eliminates value as a primary ingredient inevitably smuggles it back again by making sensations or impulses, as such, the seat of value; whereas value comes into existence through man's primordial need to distinguish between life-maintaining and life-destroying processes, and to distribute his interests and his energies accordingly" (p. 270). The historian would probably have no great quarrel with this. But a discussion would probably arise out of the question of what the so-called "values" actually have been historically.

This is not the place to discuss theories of "values." But it can probably be accepted as an axiom that life itself is one sort of value, at all times and in all places; that food is another; and that reproduction is another. But these values, accepted as axiomatic, are shared in their entirety by the other animals as well as man; there is nothing in them to distinguish man from the lower animals. The values that distinguish man from the lower animals are the more refined ones that are derived by man from these basic three. But historically, the derived values vary from place to place and from epoch to epoch. What we call the "human," or "derived," values are, indeed, derived from man's conceptions of what are the "life-maintaining" and "life-destroying" experiences for the individual or the group. The historian would differ with Mumford only in his insistence that, historically, these conceptions, these human "values," have varied enormously from one epoch to another, from place to place, and from individual to individual. (Parenthetically, it might be remarked that this freedom of the individual to differ is itself one of the most precious—and recent—values of the democratic age in Western civilization.)

The historical method imposes upon the historian the duty of trying to interpret each age in terms of its own experiences and its own values. Arnold Toynbee, seeking the reasons for the rise and decline of civilizations, finds, apparently, that the decline of a civilization takes place because of an insoluble conflict between rival sets of values within the given civilization. Mumford, apparently, attributes the decline of civilizations in the past to the failures of those civilizations to maintain a set of values that are Mr. Mumford's own. Kahler, on the other hand, defines the fundamental values of our civilization as "love and brotherhood among men." But it would be easy for the historian to show that "love" and "brotherhood among men" have never, at any time, been widely accepted in actual behavior by any considerable body of men, either within the Christian Era and area or outside of it, and least of all, perhaps, in our own time. The "values" of the Athenians and the Spartans can be documented historically. But the two sets of values, though they differed widely from each other, apparently served their purpose in both cases. And no one, probably, would accept all the Athenian values—as, for example, those attached to human slavery—as valid for us now. Yet values, to be recognized as values—that is, universal, human values—must, by definition, be applicable to every time and place. And the historian would be hard put to it to find any single human "value"—perhaps not even life, food, and reproduction—that would appear to other historians as clearly meeting this test.

Kahler gets around this dilemma by his doctrine of evolution, by which he seems to imply that values change, to be sure, but only in the course of evolution—as the primitive values of a child emerge into the mature values of the adult. But the acceptance of such a doctrine requires us to believe that modern man is actually superior to primitive or ancient man in his commonly held values. That may, of course, be the case; but the most casual glance at the present condition of man in Russia, China, Germany, India, South America, and even the United States will indicate how difficult it would be to document that fact historically—unless one is willing to accept the obvious superiority of modern Western man in material things as an index—which neither Mumford nor Kahler is willing to do.

This is, of course, not to say that values do not exist. It is merely to say that, so far as the historical record goes to show, human or derived values change; that a "value" that is "life-maintaining" in one civilization may not be so in another. Nor is it to suggest that the study of history does not teach values that are of great validity for our civilization. For it should be clear that the study of the history of civilization ought to cultivate in the student the values of criticism and tolerance, as well as to inspire in him, if only by example, a faith in the human capacity for nobility, creativeness, and service.

The professional historian, however, cannot as yet give any serious adherence to the sort of history-writing that purports to teach some preconceived sort of eternal human values, even in the interest of making his history "interesting" or "vital" for his audience. History has a method of investigation and criticism which uncompromisingly requires that every fact be documented in every possible way. The libido, the ego, and the superego, either as historical facts or as major determinants of history, have not yet been sufficiently documented. Nor has what Kahler calls the "human spirit." Nor has the concept of a set of universal, eternal, human values. What both these men, in fact, appear to propose is two new brands of humanism as religion. And this the historian, whose method still is essentially scientific and rationalistic, is unable, logically, to accept as history.

This new faith in vague, undefined values, this new type of humanism, based upon the nonrational elements in human nature, is finding its way into higher education. Indeed, it has an educational philosophy of its own, and both Mumford and Kahler give expression to their own particular variants of this philosophy. Mumford's version runs like this:

> Science itself now [today] moves toward the recovery of the subjective: part of the renewal of interest in the organic and the human. Having by strenuous self-elimination achieved objectivity with respect to the external world, man must now by an equally rigorous discipline achieve a complementary subjectivity, by a renewed command of the inner world. Instead of freezing out feelings, emotions, internal states, he must utilize them more intensively and rationally: only so can he do full justice to all the dimensions of human experience. This healing of the split personality of modern man is today one of the critical tasks of education [opposite p. 247].

Kahler's position is not unlike that of Mumford:

> In pursuing its rational and experimental methods, natural science is transcending the sphere of the rational, it has arrived at dissolving concrete matter, at questioning the unrestricted validity of "laws of nature" and of the principle of causality; its grasp is reaching the borders of the super-rational..... In this gravest of human crises, nothing is more urgent, nothing more vital than the knowledge of man, of his vast historical background and the direc-

tion of his evolution, of his distinct nature and position in the universe, in a word, of the idea of man as shown by the totality of his existence [pp. 638-39].

That there is need for a study of the entire man there can be no doubt. That the history of Western civilization, therefore, in broad but comprehensive outline should be understood by every educated man is being recognized in practice by an increasing number of colleges and universities. But for the university to abandon the rational educational method of strict historical criticism in the human sciences in the interest of developing personality in some particular way or of giving more room for play to the influence of the nonrational upon human behavior would—by all rationalists, at least—be thought dangerous in the extreme. No educator, of course, would deny the desirability of the cultivation of personality; one can only ask whether that is the prime objective of a university. Historically, the prime purpose of the university has been the discovery of truth and its propagation, and not (except indirectly) the cultivation of personality. The abandonment of this prime purpose in the interest of teaching values or morality or of developing personality as a primary function would be the abandonment of the first purpose of the university's existence—a purpose which is itself primarily and essentially rationalistic. Certain absurdities already have resulted in our intellectual life from the rediscovery of the nonrational elements in man. In the words of J. Huizinga:

> We have all long since outgrown the belief in a tyrannically consistent rationalism. We realize that not everything can be measured by reason. The advance of thought itself has brought us this realisation. A richer and deeper understanding than the solely rational has given greater meaning to our knowledge. But where the wise man, through freer and ampler judgment, finds a deeper sense in things and life, the fool finds in this freedom only license for greater nonsense. It is a truly tragic consequence: in the process of realising the limitations of reason the modern mind has

become susceptible to absurdities to which it had long been immune.[6]

The trend toward anti-intellectualism in education has been clearly noted, also, by Henry M. Wriston:

> It is difficult to realize how powerful and how widespread has been the revolt against reason in our time..... Disbelief in the potency of reason as a decisive factor in historical development and in the determination of contemporary policy is widespread, and it is deep seated.....
> The effect of anti-intellectualism upon education was notable. Learning was described as the formation of habits, the cultivation of standard responses to definite, controlled stimuli. Training in "skills," not the discipline of the mind through logical processes, was proposed as the central factor in the educational regime. In fact, the discipline of reason was ridiculed.[7]

Now it is, perhaps, desirable that some agency in the university attempt to acquaint the student with the values that have had validity in the past and with those that have currency in the present. Such an effort is now being made, indeed, in the courses in the history of Western civilization and the courses that seek to deal analytically with our contemporary civilization. But when educators begin to suggest that the universities teach "values," there is a real danger that it may mean the teaching of some particular set of values; and when these advocates, drawing distinctions between the humanities and science or complaining that the age of scientific materialism has destroyed the values that make for human happiness, rule science out of the consideration of values entirely, as Mumford and Kahler tend to do, it apparently means that they think that the values to be taught are discoverable by intuition or a sort of mysticism but not by science.

The historian, as an educator, will probably be unwilling to dilute any of the canons of historical criticism in the name of

[6] *In the Shadow of Tomorrow*, trans. by J. H. Huizinga (New York, 1936), p. 83.

[7] *Strategy of Peace* (Boston, 1944), pp. 28 and 31.

such education. He will accept the limitations upon reason described to him by the scientists in psychology. But he will be distrustful of any educational system that does not submit "hunch" or "intuition," either in the teacher or in the pupil, to rigid scientific verification. Reason alone is probably not enough, but how much less so is intuition alone! The dangers of the intuitive way in education have been amply documented by the school of Adolf Hitler. Reason remains, and probably must remain, the most trustworthy guide we have in the realm of education, which is, more than it is anything else, a search for an understanding of rationally demonstrable truth.

The two books under discussion, then, are in their own ways typical of a mood that pervades the writings of a large number of contemporary commentators on man and his history. This is a mood which, if not one of distrust of human intelligence or reason as a guide and index to human conduct and, therefore, history, at least tends to relegate reason to a role of secondary importance. These authors, like many others of our contemporaries, apparently disappointed over the failure of the age of reason quickly to bring about the millennium, tend to enthrone intuition in reason's place of leadership in human affairs. This they do, as Gerald Heard put it,[8] in an effort to bring Read and Spencer together—to restore, in other words, the nonrational elements in human behavior to the recognition, in humanistic thinking, that they deserve. Huizinga says of the current mood in general:

> The brakes of criticism are slipping. . . . It is undeniable that with the renewed desire for synthesis in the social sciences, in itself a healthy and beneficial reaction against the excessive analysis of a preceding period, the "hunch" has come to play a growing part in scientific production. There is an unending succession of bold syntheses, often constructed with great skill and erudition, in which the "originality" of the author enjoys greater triumphs than would seem compatible with sober-minded science. The social philosopher

[8] *Op. cit.,* p. 13.

[151]

sometimes assumes the role of the *bel esprit* of former ages, but it is often not quite clear whether in so doing he takes himself seriously, though he certainly intends to be taken seriously by his readers. The result is something which stands in between cultural philosophy and cultural phantasy. A strong tendency towards aesthetic forms of expression often adds still more to the confused character of the product.[9]

One might be permitted to speculate, at this point, on the question whether this new romanticism will come to dominate as large a proportion of our thinking and our aesthetic life as did the romanticism of the early nineteenth century; and, if so, whether it will be succeeded, as that one was, by a new era of realism and rationalism. It seems fair to doubt whether the attack of the new romanticism upon rationalism will succeed in the long run. If the "dynamic school of psychologists" is correct in what it tells us of the human mind, it seems reasonable to suppose that conscious intelligence will continue to be recognized as the dominant, if not the most powerful, element in historic human behavior. The extreme form of the present mood may be described as essentially backward-looking, as a sort of intellectual primitivism.

[9] *Op. cit.,* pp. 89-90.

THE PHILOSOPHY OF THE GENERAL

TOYNBEE VERSUS THE NATURALISTS

THE FINAL completion, some thirty-odd years after its conception, of Arnold Toynbee's magnum opus, *A Study of History*,[1] should probably be regarded as one of the major events in the intellectual history of the twentieth century. It is certainly one of the most monumental single-handed achievements in twentieth-century historiography.

It is a great work in many ways. It is a systematic and exhaustive *summa* of one philosophy of history—a philosophy which, while it is unique and peculiar to its author, bears a distinct kinship to Augustine's *City of God*—one that rests upon a phenomenal knowledge of history itself. Its sustained English prose may earn it a place among the classics of historical writing for its literary merits alone. Above all, however, it is a monumental religious tract—and herein lies, probably, its greatest significance—a bold, personal, highly subjective declaration of a reasoned faith for the times; a genuinely "ecumenical" faith, historically based, that transcends in many ways the provincialism of a merely Western Christianity.

---

[1] Arnold J. Toynbee, *A Study of History* (10 vols. London: Oxford University Press, for the Royal Institute of International Affairs. Vols. I-III, 1934; IV-VI, 1939; VII-X, 1954. An atlas volume is yet to appear).

As Toynbee explains in the little pamphlet that accompanies the last four volumes, *What the Book Is For; How the Book Took Shape,* his purposes in writing it were three: First,

> The balance [between the study of history in detail and the study of it as a whole] is always fluctuating and is therefore always needing to be readjusted; and, in the generation in which I happen to have been born, most Western historians have been throwing most of their weight into the study of details.... It has been a generation in which historians have had keener eyes for the trees than for the wood.... I have felt a vocation to do something, in my own work, to help to bring the wood back into focus.

As his second purpose, Toynbee intended to achieve "a synoptic view" of all "the civilizations that have been brought into our ken by the separate achievements of the archeologists, the Orientalists, and the archivists." His third purpose was a practical one:

> While, in the field of historical study, the archivists, Orientalists, and archeologists have still been working almost out of touch with one another, in the field of practical life the World has suddenly been linked up into a single world-wide society by the technicians' feat of "annihilating distance."... An historian ... can help his fellow men of different civilizations to become more familiar with one another, and, in consequence, less afraid of one another and less hostile to one another, by helping them to understand and appreciate one another's histories and to see in these local and partial stories a common achievement and common possession of the whole human family.... I do believe that a synoptic view of History is one of the World's present practical needs.

Toynbee's first problem, as he approached the task of presenting "a synoptic view" of the "common achievement and common possession of the whole human family," was the problem of defining the units or "fields" that, taken together, constitute the whole of human history. "Is there," he asks, "some intelligible field of historical study which is absolute and not merely relative to the particular social environment of particular historians?"[2] He finds such an "intelligible field of historical

[2] *Ibid.,* I, 15-16.

study" in that "species" of human society known as civilization. Of these, he discovers, in the entirety of history, twenty-one; of these twenty-one, five are "still alive." The others are dead.

His study therefore begins at the moment when "civilization," as distinguished from that other "species" called "primitive societies," appeared. He does not attempt to explain why this "species" (civilization) appeared on the earth. "The geneses of civilizations," he says, "... are particular beats of a general rhythmical pulsation which runs all through the Universe. Evidently this is as far as we can go in understanding how the geneses of civilizations occur."[3] Having isolated "civilizations" as the "species" of phenomena that he would study, and having assumed their "geneses" without attempting to explain them, he has undertaken to explain the rise, flowering, and decline of civilizations, their successions and interrelationships, and their positions relative to some great unifying principle.

Following this over-all plan, the *Study* is divided into thirteen Parts; but these logically fall into five groups. Thus, after the Introduction (Part I) the first four Parts (Parts II-V, Volumes I–VI) are concerned with the genesis, growth, breakdown, and disintegration of civilizations, considered comparatively; Parts VI, VII and VIII (Volumes VII and VIII, 1–87) are devoted to analysis of "Universal States," "Universal Churches," and "Heroic Ages," the three major factors in the decline of civilization; Parts IX and X (Volume VIII, 88-629 and IX, 1-166) are concerned with contacts between civilizations, in space and, secondly, in time; Part XI (Volume IX, 167-405) is an essay of a generalizing sort on the problem of "Law and Freedom in History"; Part XII (Volume IX, 406–644) is a speculative application of the whole philosophy to our contemporary Western civilization. The final Part of the *Study* (Part XIII, Volume X, 1–144), devoted to the historian and his *metier,* is at once a brilliant study of some of the world's greatest historians of civilization and a

3 *Ibid.,* I, 205.

highly subjective statement of Toynbee's own religious and mystical historian's faith.

Now that the work is complete, it is possible to see the pattern of history, as Toynbee conceives it, whole.

To begin with, civilizations appear as responses to challenges, internal or external. Each one grows as a result of the work of a "creative minority" within it which enjoys the confidence and the "mimesis" of the "internal proletariat." It breaks up when the "dominant minority" loses the confidence of the "internal proletariat," and there ensues a "time of troubles" which is followed by a "universal state" established by the "dominant minority" in order to preserve its own hold upon power. Disintegration follows as a result of the alienation of the "internal proletariat" from the "dominant minority"; and this process may be accelerated by the presence of an "external proletariat"—or barbarians—living beyond the borders of the "universal state."

The "primary civilizations"—Egyptiac, Sumeric, Indus culture, Shang culture, *et al.*—performed their chief historic function when they provided a groundwork for the building of the "secondary civilization"—Babylonic and Syriac, Indic, Sinic, Hellenic, *et al.* From the disintegration of these civilization of the "second generation" were derived the four great "higher religions," or "churches"—Hinduism, Mahayana Buddhism, Christianity, and Islam. These churches constitute "a higher species of society." The "third-generation" civilizations, of which our "post-modern" Western civilization is one, "were derived from the secondary through higher religions providing chrysalis-churches; [now], the internal proletariats of disintegrating tertiary civilizations [have] been creating the rudiments of higher religions of a new generation—rudiments, whose genesis was, at the time of writing [*ca.* A.D. 1952], an accomplished fact, though their prospects were still obscure."[4]

4 *Ibid.*, VII, 422. There appears to be a distinct shift of thought and of mood between the first six volumes (Parts I-V), published prior to the Second

The Philosophy of the General

Such is the rhythm of the history of civilizations and churches. But this explanation of the rhythm of history is not yet, for Toynbee, a sufficient explanation of the whole of the process of history. Such an explanation must also include the nature and significance of contacts between civilizations, because civilizations do rise and fall and do influence each other, either by contacts between contemporaries (civilizations of the same generation) or by influence through "apparentation" and "affiliation" (between civilizations of different generations). But the cyclical rises and falls of civilizations are as the turning of the wheels of a cart that is moving uphill. The cart is the symbol of the Soul of Man, or the Souls of Men, marching ever upward toward the ultimate aim of Man, which is "fellowship with the One True God." It is for this reason that the histories of civilizations are meaningless without the unifying and significance-giving religious element, the history of the progress of the Soul of Man toward God.

When Toynbee applies this line of reasoning to the "postmodern," or "tertiary," "westernizing" civilization of the world of the mid-twentieth century (Part XII),[5] it is not surprising that he should not only find that the Western civilization has already passed through five hundred years of a "time of troubles" and faces the prospect of a new and world-wide "universal state," to be achieved either by forceful imposition by Russia and its allies or by the United States and its own, or by the voluntary formation of some sort of world-wide state coöperatively by the two presently opposing camps. This formation of a universal state, of course, is

World War, and the last four volumes (Parts VI-XIII) published some fifteen years later. For the latter parts, and especially Parts VII-XIII, are much more deeply and explicitly religious in outlook. Toynbee himself, in fact, comes to the conclusion (whether newly or consistently with his original plan) that the study of the "species" of society known as civilizations, as presented in Volumes I-VI, is in itself fruitless, and that the pattern of history becomes intelligible only by studying the "universal churches" as a "higher species of society." This idea does not seem to appear, at least explicitly, in the first six volumes.

[5] *Ibid.*, IX, 406-644.

a fore-symptom of eventual disintegration; out of this disintegration may come a new "higher religion" that will fuse the four great extant "higher religions" into one. This higher religion, too, will be the highest stage of civilization to have been reached by mankind up to that time.

This new religion may be built upon the basic common denominator of all the four great extant higher religions, which is their monotheistic concept of God. But this development is not certain; for Man is free to err. Twentieth-century man, in fact, is presently faced by a great choice: he may choose to worship himself, because of the spectacular successes of his science and industry, or he may choose the true worship, the worship of the One True God.

This freedom to choose derives from the fact that Man is subject to the operation of two sorts of laws in history (Part XI),[6] "natural law" and the "law of God." As an animal, man is bound by natural law, including the law of his own nature, as other animals; but as a human soul he is free: for the law of God is the law of freedom. Thus man is free to choose, under the divine law, even the ways that may lead to his own destruction. For this reason the prospect of the "post-modern," "westernizing" civilization may not be predicted with assurance.

Such is the pattern of history seen as a whole as it emerges in this monumental study. As an explanation of the nature and the "meaning behind the facts"; he is also a poet. For in seeking the only of history but of human existence as well. And it is a religious philosophy. For the true progress of mankind is here not, in fact, in civilizations but in religion: in the hierarchy of values, a "higher religion" is a stage of human progress superior to that represented by civilizations. This leads ineluctably to the conclusion that, for Toynbee, the rise and creative flowering of a civilization is of less historic significance than its disintegration; since out of the disintegration of the "primary civilizations" came

---

6 *Ibid.*, IX, 167-405.

the higher "secondary civilizations"; and the newer and brighter
"higher religion" of the future will, presumably, derive from the
disintegration of the civilization of the present.

What, then, in this pattern, or perspective, is history itself?
For Toynbee,

> History [was] a vision—dim and partial, yet (he believed) true to
> reality as far as it went—of God revealing Himself in action to Souls
> that were sincerely seeking Him. ... History's contribution is to
> give us a vision of God's creative activity on the move in a frame
> which, in our human experience of it, displays six dimensions.
> The historical angle of vision shows us the physical cosmos moving
> centrifugally in a four-dimensional frame of Space-Time; it shows
> us Life on this planet moving evolutionarily in a five-dimensional
> frame of Life-Time-Space; and it shows us human souls, raised to a
> sixth dimension by the gift of the Spirit, moving, through a fateful
> exercise of their spiritual freedom, either towards their Creator or
> away from Him.[7]

This is the dynamic vision that is history, and the historian, for
Toynbee, is one who, having "had the happiness of having an aim
in life, has found his vocation in a call from God to 'feel after Him
and find Him.' "[8] But the scholar must go beyond a mere feeling
after God: he must follow his vocation into action and the artis-
tic creativity of writing history. "A scholar is proving himself
guilty of a subconscious hypocrisy to which he is wilfully shutting
his mind's eye," he says, "when he pleads guilty of ignorance and
protests that his conscience will not permit him to publish, write,
or even say anything on his subject until he has mastered the last
jot and tittle of the information available up to date."[9] A historian is thus by vocation a searcher after God and a publisher of
his findings—in short, a sort of priest of the religion of history.

But the true subject-matter of history is not, and cannot be,
merely a fragment of the whole. Like Herodotus, Ibn Khaldun,
and others, Toynbee comes to the conclusion that "no field smaller
than the entire *Oikoumenê* since the dawn of Civilization is an

[7] *Ibid.*, X, 102.   [8] *Ibid.*, X, 1.   [9] *Ibid.*, X, 26.

intelligible field of historical study."[10] His constant problem is, "how has this come out of that?" And no answer based upon part of the *Oikoumenê* can be more than a partial, and, therefore, a distorted answer.

Toynbee scolds the modern historians for being satisfied to study fragments of the whole history, and for the consequent relativity of their thinking.[11] He also scolds them for their "antinomianism"—for their refusal to admit that there is law in human history,[12] and especially for their "repudiation of a belief in a 'Law of God.' "[13] And in a provocative and amusing parable of the ducks (historians) and the seagulls (social scientists) he ridicules the "know-nothing" attitude of the historians which permits the aggressiveness of the social scientists to seize upon the most succulent morsels of historical study, in the formulation of generalizations and the laws of human behavior.[14]

The matter of the study of history is, then, the entire *Oikoumenê* and the laws that govern it. But it is to be remembered that the laws are of two kinds, "natural law" and the "law of God." The laws of nature are to be sought in the facts; the laws of God are to be found in the meaning behind the facts. And this meaning, it appears, is to be found in the subconscious area of the mind, or "psyche":

> for the Subconscious, not the Intellect, is the organ through which Man lives his spiritual life for good or evil. It is the fount of Poetry, Music, and the Visual Arts, and the channel through which the Soul is in Communion with God when it does not steel itself against God's influence.[15]

The first step in the investigation of the "meaning behind the facts" should be "to seek insight into the working of the Heart"; the second should be "to explore the nature of the difference between rational truth and intuitive truth, in the belief that each of them is genuine Truth—though each only in its own sphere,

10 *Ibid.*, X, 80.   12 *Ibid.*, IX, 173-219.   14 *Ibid.*, IX, 193-194.
11 *Ibid.*, I, 1-16.   13 *Ibid.*, IX, 217.   15 *Ibid.*, VII, 500.

and only as far as it goes." The third step should be to seek "to strike the underlying rock of fundamental Truth on which rational and intuitive truth alike must be founded. And the final objective, in striving to strike rock-bottom in the psychic cosmos, would be to attain to a fuller vision of God the Dweller in the Innermost."[16]

Finally, the historian is not only a scholar concerned with investigating "the relations between the facts of History" and the "meaning behind the facts"; he is also a poet. For in seeking the relations between the facts "we are [only] trying to see God through History with our intellects"; but "the Intellect . . . is only one faculty of the Soul"; another faculty, which must be used by the historian, is "the feelings." For "feelings about History, as well as thoughts about it, have inspired historical works, and similar feelings, evoked by similar facts, have also been expressed in imaginative works in the divers genres of literature."[17] Thus,

> the meaning behind the facts of History towards which the poetry in the facts is leading us is a revelation of God and a hope of communion with Him. . . .[18] When the feeling for the poetry in the facts of History is thus transmuted into awe at the epiphany of God in History, the historian's inspiration is preparing him for an experience that has been described as "the Beatific Vision" by souls to whom it has been vouchsafed. In this experience, God is seen face to face, and no longer through a glass darkly; and this means that the vision carries the Soul beyond the limits of History or of any other avenue of approach towards God through His revelation of His nature in His works. Yet, for every seeker after God, his own God-given glimpse of the marvels of the Created Universe . . . is a lamp unto his feet and a light unto his path; and the historian's path ascends from a feeling for the poetry in History through a sense of awe at God's action in History to a participation in Man's fellowship with Man which brings him to the threshold of the saint's communion with God.[19]

This is a sort of historico-religious, poetic mysticism.

Another aspect of this same mystical approach to history is the

16 *Ibid.*, VII, 500-501.   18 *Ibid.*, X, 126.
17 *Ibid.*, X, 113.   19 *Ibid.*, X, 129.

mystic empathy of the historian for the events he will describe. This involves a sort of transport in which the historian seems to find himself in the actual presence of the events. Such, for example, were several of Toynbee's own experiences—such as one which gave him "an abiding sense of personal participation in the War of 90–80 B.C. between Rome and her Italian allies. . . ."[20]

It is upon this high religious and mystical note that *A Study of History* ends. The closing passage is a quotation from the *Te Deum* and Toynbee's own litany addressed to all those spirits, secular and religious, pagan and Christian, human and divine, that have assisted human souls forward in their progress through history toward God:

Christe, audi nos.
Christ Tammuz, Christ Adonis, Christ Osiris, Christ Balder, hear us, by whatsoever name we bless Thee for suffering death for our salvation. . . .

Buddha Gautama, show us the path that will lead us out of our afflictions. . . .

Mother Mary, Mother Isis, Mother Cybele, Mother Ishtar, Mother Kwanyin, have compassion on us. . . .

Noble Lucretius, who, in spite of thyself, art also a forerunner of the Saviour, instil thy poetry into our hearts and thy sincerity into our understandings. . . .

Valiant Zarathustra. . . .

Tender-hearted Muhammad. . . .

Blessed Mo-Ti, disciple of Christ before Christ's epiphany in a far country. . . .

Omnes Sancti et Sanctae Dei, intercedite pro nobis;

For *ilayhi marji'ukum jami'an:* to Him return ye every one.[21]

Unquestionably, Arnold Toynbee has constructed one of the

[20] *Ibid.*, X, 130.   [21] *Ibid.*, X, 143-144.

most magnificent historical *summae* ever written by single individuals. But many Western historians, especially the rationalists among them, will reject Toynbee's philosophy and his subjective, emotional historiography on several major grounds.

In the first place, they will reject his extreme subjectivity. He gives lip service to empiricism, and when he treats of historic civilizations, upon the basis of empirical sources (especially in Volumes I-VI), his history writing and his empiricism are brilliantly successful. It can be said, indeed, that his demonstration of natural law in human history, resting, as it does, upon empirical evidence, is very substantially grounded, and would be difficult to refute. But in his treatment of the "Soul" and "The One True God," he makes a leap of faith that a historian insisting upon empirical evidence cannot follow. That there is poetry in history, of course, can be agreed. But that there is a poetic license for the historian to soar far beyond his empirically verifiable data for the enjoyment of a wholly subjective "beatific vision" the empirical historian could never admit.

Furthermore, and by the same token, the empirically-minded historian must reject, as history, Toynbee's evangelical homiletics. For history is not an evangel calling men to repent and be saved, as this *Study,* in considerable measure, is. One of history's most important aspects, to be sure, is its nature as an effort, based upon the empirical record, to understand the nature of man and his place in the universe; as such it is clearly a form of philosophy. But to remain history it must retain, at all costs, its objectivity and its empirical nature. Its use as a gospel of salvation to rationalize a subjective, poetic, and religious mysticism completely denatures it as history and transforms it into mystical religious poetry.

In the second place, Toynbee's interpretation of Western history since the withdrawal of Rome from Gaul and Spain indicates a conviction that no real progress has been made in the West since the advent of Christianity there. If the children of the

[163]

Western civilization, he says, could think of the rise of Western secular society as being

> one of the "vain repetitions of the heathen"—an almost meaningless repetition of something that the Hellenes had done before them, and done supremely well—then the greatest new event in the historical background of a Modern Western Society would be seen to be a very different one. The greatest new event would then not be the monotonous rise of yet another secular civilization out of the bosom of the Christian Church in the course of these latter centuries; it would still be the Crucifixion and the Crucifixion's spiritual consequences.[22]

The fact is that Toynbee accepts the evidence of the inspirations of ancient prophets and seers as superior to the empirical evidence of modern science. Both are evidence, of course; but to him the evidence of the "intuitive truth" of the prophets is superior to empirical, rational, scientific truth. Modern historians will find it impossible to accept "intuitive truth" as evidence of anything beyond the individual experience of the person whose intuitive experience it is.

But the most substantial critique of Toynbee may probably come from the naturalist or "anthropological" school of historian-philosophers. These, indeed, will find much in Toynbee to admire and much with which to agree.

They will start, of course, with an acceptance of the position that man is, as a matter of scientific fact, subject to natural law. But they will also maintain that, as a biological organism, the product of evolution, man is distinguished from other organisms only by the fact that, as a result of a long series of fortuitous mutations of the human genes, this animal has a higher degree of intelligence—or reason—than they. History, in this context, is the record of man—or outstanding men of genius—thinking, and of the results of this thinking in action.

Curiously enough, the anthropological school of historians would probably accept practically the same terms that Toynbee

[22] *Ibid.,* VII, 446-447.

does, in explanation of both cultures and civilizations. For thinking, to them, is a biological response to a challenge; and all the mechanisms of culture and civilization, including religion, are devices for survival that man has invented, by his thinking, in response to the challenges that have confronted him.

The anthropological historian would go further. For he would accept the general idea that civilizations or cultures progress as long as they are creative and encourage creativity, but that they tend to stagnate and decline when a minority controlling society succeeds in arresting creativity in the interest of perpetuating, in a fixed and unchangeable *status quo,* a set of ideas and institutions which, in the original era of creativity, have proved their validity as successful responses to the challenges then facing the civilization.[23]

The rationalists will also admit, probably, that within certain biological limits, man is free. This freedom, however, is not, to them, the freedom of the "law of God," nor is it evidence of any intervention of anything supernatural in human affairs. This freedom is a biological phenomenon, purely and simply—a freedom which is evidence only that the evolution of this organism has proceeded to the point where it is free consciously to choose among alternative ways of action and even to plan its own further biological evolution.

These historians will reject the cyclical interpretation of the rises and falls of civilizations in its entirety. That there are "creative" periods and "stagnant" or "static" or "noncreative" periods in a civilization's history they will, of course, concede; but it is beyond their credence to assert, for example, that the Han era and the T'ang era in China represented two separate and distinct civilizations, or that the Maurya and Gupta periods in India or the Old Kingdom and the Empire in Egypt did. Nor can the empirical historian speak, in the light of all the evidence, of

[23] Compare, for example, A. L. Kroeber, *Configurations of Culture Growth* (Berkeley, 1944), especially Chapter XI.

"renaissances" as simply "contacts between civilizations in time"; nor can he accurately say that the so-called "Italian renaissance" was either purely Italian or a true renaissance; he would insist, most especially and emphatically, that that so-called "renaissance," to him, does not represent a true "repetition," "revival," or "re-birth" of "Hellenic" (Greco-Roman) civilization.

On the contrary, the empiricist-historian might probably maintain a sort of rectilinear theory of civilizations, admitting, even in Toynbee's own terms, that the presence of a challenge, or combination of challenges, might provoke responses in the form of creative activity and "growth," and that the absence of challenge, especially where a fixed and relatively unchanging *status quo* is deliberately maintained, has generally resulted in a decline of creativity and consequent absence of "growth." But he probably would insist that even these apparent "pulsations" may not be necessary, provided only that the constantly changing problems of society present constantly new challenges to creative minds and that men themselves maintain their minds free of restraint and alert to the possibility of new creativity.

There is a unity of existence, too, in the naturalist-historian's view. But the unity of existence is the basic atomic unity of matter. The biologist tells us that man is made of atomic matter, like everything else in the universe, and that his behavior is only the behavior of that same stuff in a certain highly specialized and complex form.

Thus the various types of human behavior may not be tagged as "sin" and "righteousness." The conscious individual[24] and the social aggregate of individuals use intelligence—or reason—in the constant effort to control impulses that may have undesirable results and to encourage those which are likely to have desirable ones. And the subconscious, far from being the seat of human "wisdom" or the avenue of the "Soul's" communication with God,

[24] *Cf.* Herbert J. Muller, *The Uses of the Past* (New York, 1952), Chapter 3, *et passim.*

is merely the seat of mental control (partially, but only partially, subject to conscious intelligence) for such quasi-automatic biological functions as hunger or the sex impulse. The line between subconscious impulse and purely intelligent choice or planning is not sharply drawn; what can be said with a fair degree of assurance is that, biologically, the intelligence is a mechanism for solving problems that cannot be solved by purely automatic or partially automatic—reflex or conditioned-reflex—reactions.

History, in this biological or anthropological perspective, is the process and the record of humanity behaving under the direction of a complex combination of mental functions; intellectual history, at least, seems to be simply the history of men thinking. If this be true, then both the "good" that men have done and the "evil" are man's own responsibility, not God's. The Parthenon, the Taj Mahal, the Gothic Cathedral, the Grand Coulee Dam, or the use of atomic fission for peace as well as for war, are all irrefutable empirical evidences of man's intelligence at work. Similarly, the destruction of millions of lives and uncounted and uncountable books and *objets d'art* in the name of nationalism, dynastic power, or religion, are also empirical evidence of man's intelligence at work. One set of evidence shows choices of ways of action that were beneficial for men; the second set of evidence reveals choices that were not ultimately beneficial, constitutes evidence chiefly that the human intelligence may err as to what is beneficial.

Thus, all that has happened occurred within an entirely naturalistic universe, and the anthropologist-historian would be compelled to reject supernatural phenomena along with intuitive truth. He would reject, above all, any subjective, intuitive, or mystical religious explanation of human history, because, as a historian who may not go beyond his empirically verifiable data, he would be compelled to say "no evidence."

History, in the last analysis, is, and must be, a rigorously empirical study. It rests squarely upon empirically verifiable

[167]

evidence and no other. Any study that ignores existing empirical evidence, or invents subjective evidence to suit its preconceived assumptions, or embarks upon poetic flights of fantasy without any evidence whatsoever, is not history.

It is conceivable that Arnold Toynbee may prove to be the prophet of a new era in the intellectual and spiritual life of mankind. For in his noble vision of a truly "ecumenical" religion for all humanity he does seem to voice the aspirations of what must be a very large proportion of the articulate members of our "Westernizing Society"; and he gives it as an axiom "that all historical thought is inevitably relative to the particular circumstances of the thinker's own time and place."[25] If his suggestions as to the possible future developments of civilization and religion should prove to be even roughly accurate, he will go down in history and in the history of history as one of the most perspicacious minds of all time.

On the other hand, *A Study of History* may prove to be an anachronism, a book, essentially backward-looking, that seeks to rationalize the failures of religion into the terms of an indomitable and unquenchable faith that is at once unhistorical, because divorced from empirical evidence, irrational, and "rationally" defiant of reason itself. If the biological-anthropological historians are closer to empirical data and, therefore, to historical reality, then they, and not Toynbee, are really the true voice of history in the twentieth century. In that case, this *meister werk* must become but the most eloquent of all the voices of those who are still living in an age of faith that is past, who are not at home, and who, therefore, are not happy, in the atomic, relativistic universe revealed by science—a universe of which they are integral parts but which knows them not.

[25] *A Study of History,* III, 476.

HISTORIAN'S PROGRESS

OR

THE QUEST FOR SANCTA SOPHIA

FIFTY YEARS after the event, Historicus could vividly remember seeing, as a child of about ten, the great Theodore Roosevelt go down the main street of his home town in an open, horse-drawn carriage—top-silk hat, pince-nez, bushy, toothy smile, and all. He could remember the occasion, during the election of 1908, when he was jostled off the sidewalk by a noisy group of young Republican electioneers in a town that was about ninety per cent Democratic, "croaking for Taft" with small metal gadgets which, when pressed, emitted a hoarse, croaking noise. He could clearly remember reading the newspaper accounts of the Democratic party convention of 1912, when he had been stirred by the long-drawn-out battle for the nomination between Champ Clark and that knight in shining armor, that Galahad who "had the strength of ten because his heart was pure," Woodrow Wilson. Historicus was now sixteen, and his first great living hero was Woodrow Wilson. And when Wilson visited his home town to make the famous "Mobile Speech" in 1913, he played hooky from his $1.00-a-week job in the drugstore and slipped into the Lyric Theatre without a ticket to hear the great man speak. Three months after he turned twenty-one, the United States entered the First World War—the vastest and most destructive and, it may be, the most

[169]

critical and decisive that the world, up to that time, had ever seen.

Perhaps this conditioning in his youth directed Historicus to take up the Quest. Perhaps, also, Historicus, sprung from a long line of hardshell Baptist forebears, felt the same crusading zeal for righteousness that his hero, Wilson, felt. Probable it does seem that the reading of much of the Arthurian cycle during these same years may have inspired in him a romantic spirit of seeking akin to that which he fancied had animated the knights of the Table Round.

Above all, it was probably the experience of being caught up into the stream of history by an engine called, in that day, the draft, and brought into direct contact with one of the major events of all time—that stupendous and horrendous war—that finally crystallized the vague and unformed curiosities of Historicus' mind into the determination to seek the meaning of things, particularly wars, in the study of their historical derivations. Why did men fight? Why was he, Historicus, caught up, with or without his consent or interest, into war? Did men cause this war and the torrent of events that came with it, or were men caught in the currents of events and forces that were already flowing with irresistible power—currents which men, it appeared, were powerless to arrest or deflect, but which, perhaps, they might hope to direct toward the lesser of two evil ends? Was there some meaning, some plan behind this apparently senseless chaos, imperceptible to the naked eye but comprehensible on the basis of a careful, objective study of its antecedents? What was the plan or pattern, if any, upon which the epic of human experience within historic times was written?

There was only one way to find the answer to these questions. He must study history. He would come, he hoped, to understand man and his destiny and his significance in the universal scheme of things, by studying what man had been and done and thought. Then, having arrived at an understanding of man by a study of man's past, he might hope, at last, to be prepared to offer reasonably intelligent or useful suggestion for the service of his fellow-men and the enrichment of men's future.

He would know the truth, for he believed the truth would make him free; he would find wisdom, for wisdom, he hoped, might make him a worthy servant of mankind.

Whatever its sources, by the time he finished his war-time hitch in the United States Navy nearly a year after the armistice of 1918, his Quest for Holy Wisdom was consciously and definitely launched.

METHOD

Once Historicus had decided that history was to be his *métier*, he set himself, more or less consciously, to master the tools, the techniques, and the materials of his trade. He placed himself under the tutelage of the old masters, past and present, and, like any other apprentice, did most of his learning of his craft "on the job." Nor could it have been otherwise; for he was to learn that no man's mastery of the tools, the techniques, and the materials of history could ever be perfect. The best he could hope for was steady improvement. There was no such thing as absolute mastery of historical method; mastery was eventually only a matter of degree.

Practically, it was not difficult to discover the uses of the tools of scholarship: bibliographies and the bibliographies of bibliographies, the making of bibliography cards, the taking of notes, and the writing of impressive footnotes and annotated bibliographies. It was not so easy to master the techniques of sharp documentary criticism and evaluation, or to take the raw material represented by hundreds or even thousands of notes and build out of it a presentable intellectual structure in the form of a fifteen or twenty-page contribution to historical knowledge. Yet, this part of his methodology, too, he did not find insuperably difficult.

Evidently the problem of method embraced much more than a mastery of the mere tools of research. Historical method also depended upon the canons governing the selection of evidence, the critical use of evidence, and the interpretation of the evidence.

For himself, Historicus was always fascinated by the temptation to generalize—to take the little lumps of pure metal turned out by the monographists and use them as building blocks to erect historical constructs on large, architectonic lines. Like Carl Becker, he was compelled to admit that, for him, "... nothing can be duller than historical facts, and nothing more interesting than the service they can be made to render in the effort to solve the everlasting riddle of human existence."[1]

There were some giants among historians, such as a Gibbon, a Ranke, or a Toynbee, who not only displayed a phenomenal intellectual capacity to seize upon the facts in vast areas of the human past, but, also, to weave those vast quantities of facts into fabrics showing clear patterns for the understanding of the nature of man and of society and of the meaning of human existence. It grew upon him gradually, but with a thrilling sense of conviction, that history, in the hands of such creative thinkers, was the true philosophy.

Historicus stood in humble consternation before the sheer vastness and power of the genius of these great historians. But his humility was tempered with arrogance. For he found that he disagreed with all of them. In his mind they were all—every one of them—wrong at least as to the patterns they discovered in their findings.

Indeed, it was all too obvious that if there was one characteristic shared by the historians of all time and all places, it was that every one disagreed with every other. The evidence presented by written history itself seemed to show that no two historians ever agreed completely on any important historical problem.

Historicus kept reminding himself that, despite the differences between historians, there were certain essential facts upon which

[1] Quoted in Charlotte W. Smith, *Carl Becker: On History and the Climate of Opinion* (Ithaca, 1956), 47.

the historians could agree; the fact, for example, that the text of the American Declaration of Independence was adopted by the Continental Congress on July 4, 1776, or the fact that Hitler's armies marched into Poland at dawn on September 1, 1939. As he considered it, the quantity of historical fact that was accepted by all historians as given, or agreed upon, turned out to be enormous. Yet he also remembered that many so-called historical "facts" had been shown *not* to be facts by the unending process of historical criticism, and that any one of them might be destroyed at any minute, as when, for example, some young student writing a dissertation on the American Revolution might show incontrovertibly that the Declaration was not signed on the fourth of July, 1776, after all. This tentativeness of historical knowledge, this constant threat that any hitherto accepted fact might at any moment be shown to be not a fact, made of the accepted body of historical knowledge emphatically nothing more than what Charles Peirce might have called a "consensus," one that was constantly being revised by continuous study.

Still, the question remained: why did historical thinkers, great or small, invariably disagree, once they got beyond the simple basic facts? Why was it so patently true that any group of historians, using approximately the same evidence for the history of a single event, would almost invariably come up with as many different explanations of the event as there were historians studying it? Or, again, why did the historians of one generation so invariably differ from those of all the generations that had preceded it?

Clearly, there was an obvious and inescapable relativism in historical knowledge. How was it to be explained? And what should Historicus' own position relative to the others be? Could this relativism ever be converted into universal certainty? And was this a problem of method merely, of the conditioning of the intellectual generation in which the historian lived, or of innate differences among the individual historians' minds?

[173]

Historicus now realized that the effort to devise a dependable historical method had carried him straight into the problem of knowledge itself. How did he know what he knew? How did he know that he knew it? And why did his own knowing differ so sharply from the knowing of everyone else?

He could start with the simple assumption that the world outside himself actually existed, at least approximately, as revealed to him by his senses and the reports of the scientists. By a similar assumption he could proceed upon the basis of a conviction that what men had done in the past had actually been done; and that the documents and artifacts left by the actors upon the stage of history constituted valid evidence that they had actually been there.

In a sense, of course, the past did not exist at all; it was lost forever. What did exist was a perception of it in the historian's mind. Yet history had happened. What had happened—the event—was completely external, or objective, to the historian. History was like the explosion of a star, now visible, that actually occurred a million years before *homo sapiens* had put in his appearance on this globe. If this were true, then the historian was nothing more than an observer, an analyzer, and an interpreter of what he saw, exactly as the astronomer was the observer and interpreter of the explosion of the star. For the astronomer, the light-waves that reached his telescope were satisfactory physical evidence that the explosion had actually taken place; for the historian, the Declaration of Independence, say, with the original signatures put there by the living men, now dead, who had signed it, was exactly comparable, as physical evidence that the Declaration had actually been made and the document had actually been signed.

It was the sum total of such events that had actually happened that Historicus called the corpus of historical fact or events. There it was; it was completely external, or objective to the historian; it could never change, no matter what the historian might do; it would remain the same, unchanged and unchangeable, though no historian had ever been born. It was only the historian's perception of it that changed.

In this sense the historian was in exactly the same position, relative to his subject-matter, that the scientist was. History itself, in this sense, was a science; and Historicus could go along with Collingwood at least far enough to agree that history

> ... is a science, but a science of a special kind. It is a science whose business is to study events not accessible to our observation, and to study these events inferentially, arguing to them from something else which is accessible to our observation, and which the historian calls "evidence" for the events in which he is interested.[2]

The first important principle, then, was that the corpus of historical events was real, and that it was objective to the historian; he was also external to it, up to the moment of his own conception, as a student of it; he was in very truth a scientist, bound by the rules of scientific objectivity.

But the second important fact was that every historical scientist differed from every other in his method and in his perception of history. Every historian's method of study included the emotional and intellectual predispositions he brought to his investigation. These things were highly subjective; it was clear, therefore, that the historian's attitude toward his subject matter powerfully influenced the use of the method and the character of the final product. Obviously, the rationalism of a Gibbon, the realism of a Ranke, or the religious mysticism of a Toynbee, brought to the study by the historian, was a preexistent frame of mind, a product, it might be, of the intellectual conditioning of the historian which gave direction to the historian's study and suffused everything he wrote. The history of Roman democracy written by a Whig historian almost certainly would be different from that written by a Tory historian.

In other words, Historicus could not escape the conclusion that,

2 R. G. Collingwood, *The Idea of History* (Oxford, 1946), 251-252.

whereas the corpus of past historical events was something given, fixed and unchanging, and external to the historian, knowledge of the factual reality could only be subjective, relative to the individual historian, and that the consensus of this historical knowledge or truth could only be relatively true or complete. It followed that historical method, at its best, could produce in the mind of the historian no more than a relatively low or high degree of truth with regard to any historical event.

Taken together, these two fundamental principles indicated that a line must be drawn between the corpus of historical fact or event which was objective, and the methodology of every individual historian, which was subjective. Even so, the problem still remained: why did the methodology of every historian, and consequently, his findings, differ from those of every other?

One of the answers to this question appeared to lie in the apparent fact that every historian's thinking is conditioned by the social and intellectual environment in which he lives. Historicus thought that Frederick Jackson Turner had been—and remained—substantially correct in his remark that "each age writes the history of the past anew with reference to the conditions uppermost in its own time. . . . This does not mean that the real events of a given age change; it means that our comprehension of these facts changes."[3]

In fact, as the intellectual currents of the twentieth century flowed on, there appeared a whole school of sociohistorical thought headed by Karl Mannheim[4] that Mannheim himself called the "Sociology of Knowledge"—one that proclaimed it as a scientific fact that all thought—and therefore, all history—is social thought; that what a man thinks, that is, the entire complex

[3] Frederick Jackson Turner, "An American Definition of History," in Fritz Stern, ed., *The Varieties of History* (New York, 1956), 200.

[4] Karl Mannheim, *Freedom, Power, and Democratic Planning* (New York, 1950), 179. See also Mannheim's *Man and Society in an Age of Reconstruction* (New York, 1940), *Ideology and Utopia* (New York, 1951), and *Diagnosis of Our Time* (New York, 1944).

of a man's thinking, is formed by the "conditioning" exercised upon him by the society in which he lives. Indeed, all human behavior, which includes thought, is in reality determined by this conditioning; it is the function of the "science of human behavior" to discover, by a rigidly scientific method, the laws governing such human behavior and thought. Once the laws of human behavior are discovered, the further step to the deliberately directed formation of human character and behavior should be a relatively short and easy one.[5]

This whole line of thinking was most arresting to Historicus because of its apparently implied denial that any of the great historical monuments created by the intelligence at work was or ever had been in fact the product of a free individual genius. It seemed to require, in effect, a revolutionary rewriting of history; for it appeared that the individual could never have created anything: all thought was social thought; all invention was social invention; all creativity was social creativity.

In his first reactions to behavioralism Historicus was inclined to write it off as a pseudoscientific, philosophical rationalization of the obvious historic fact of the twentieth-century mass mind. But he soon discovered that this could not so easily be done. Much of the evidence that the behavioralists presented was well-nigh incontrovertible. The problem, from the point of view of the historian, was to discover how much of it was sound, and in what degree it should be accepted as a legitimate mechanism in the methodology of historiography. Indeed, there was much, even in the historiography of his own time, that had the appearance of confirming the behavioralist's position.

This behavioralist mood, as expressed in an effort to devise exact scientific methods for the study of human society and the natural laws that govern its behavior, was actually not without its

---

[5] See, for example, B. F. Skinner, "Freedom and the Control of Men," *The American Scholar*, XXV, 47-65; and, by the same author, *Walden Two* (New York, 1948), 162, 243, *et passim.*

influence upon the methodology of history. Indeed, certain experiments were made by historians to test the possible validity of this new outlook for history writing, and certain essays on historical methodology both rebuked the historians for their failure to be scientific in the behavioralist sense and called upon them to devise more exact, scientific methods for the pursuit of their studies. Some even began to speak of history as a behavioral science.[6]

There did unquestionably appear to be a trend, or drift, in the thinking of the observers of the mid-twentieth century toward an acceptance of the proposition that much, if not all, thought is determined by social moods and influences. One had only to glance at the works of such writers as Erich Fromm,[7] David Riesman,[8] Alan Valentine,[9] William H. Whyte, Jr.,[10] Erich Kahler,[11] and others to see how powerful were the "collective" ways of thinking in influencing the thought and the personalities of individuals.

For himself, Historicus recognized that the behavioralist "had something." Still, although they had a part of the truth, it seemed to him that they did not have it all. They had not presented sufficient evidence, in his opinion, to compel the revolutionary denial of individual differences that seemed to be necessarily bound up with their doctrine.

The behavioralists' answer seemed, in the face of the obvious historical evidence, far too simple. There were still too many

6 See, for example, Lee Benson and Thomas Pressly, "Can Differences in Interpretations of the Causes of the Civil War be Resolved Objectively?" (Unpublished manuscript of a paper presented at the annual meeting of the American Historical Association, December, 1956). See, also, Lee Benson, "Research Problems in American Political Historiography," in *Common Frontiers of the Social Sciences*, edited by Mirra Komarovsky (Glencoe, Ill., 1957), 113-185, and Walter A. Sedelow, Jr., "History as Language" (unpublished manuscript read before the annual meeting of the American Sociological Society, 1957).

7 Erich Fromm, *Escape From Freedom* (New York, 1941).

8 David Riesman, *The Lonely Crowd* (New Haven, 1950).

9 Alan Valentine, *The Age of Conformity* (Chicago, 1954).

10 William H. Whyte, Jr., *The Organization Man* (New York, 1956).

11 Erich Kahler, *The Tower and the Abyss* (New York, 1957).

individual differences, even among historians, to permit of the acceptance of Mannheim's dictum that *"all* thinking is social thinking."

But what other evidence, if any, could be brought to bear upon this aspect of the problem of how historians know and why they differ? How, otherwise, could the obvious fact of individual intellectual differences be explained? Even the mental tests devised by the psychologists themselves seemed to confirm the apparent fact that all individuals *are* different, both in intellectual capacity and in vocational aptitude. Were these differences to be explained only in terms of social conditioning?

Historicus discovered—or thought he did—a key to the answers to these questions in the findings of certain biologists. Because according to them every human brain, and, therefore, mind, differs from every other in its *biological* composition and function. As N. S. Berrill put it,

> Humans vary in every quality of mind and spirit as well as in physique and appearance, physiology and longevity. We differ in almost everything we can think of—in sense of taste and smell, reaction to color and sound, in our ways of doing things, in all our likes and dislikes, in our allergies and susceptibilities, in femininity or masculinity. Individualism is a greater attribute of the human species than of any other kind of living organism and much of the hate so rampant in human relations stems from this essential human diversity and our failure to accept and understand it. . . . Rather than force our children along the lines of standardized sociability, fostering the illusion that they are supposed to be a uniform product of a human assembly line, we should be teaching them that the juvenile passion to be average, normal and secure is a retreat from life.[12]

This seemed, at least, to mean that according to the findings of science there is a biological basis for intellectual differences. More

12 N. S. Berrill, *Man's Emerging Mind* (New York, 1955), 247. See also Julian Huxley, *Evolution in Action* (New York, 1953) and Hermann J. Muller, "Life," in *Man's Right to Knowledge: Second series: Present Knowledge and New Directions* (New York, 1956), 19-33.

importantly, however, it seemed to lend a dependable scientific sanction to the belief that in some of its functions, at least, the human intelligence is free.

Inevitably this implied another logical question, which seemed to be answered in the affirmative by the psychological tests, whether one man's mind might have, biologically, a greater degree of freedom of function than another. If so, it meant a certain amount of biological determinism toward a greater or lesser freedom of the intelligence in individuals, with consequent effects upon the individuals' ways of thinking. Even so, it did appear that the freedom was real; that every individual human mind was in some greater or lesser degree free to direct its own behavior independently of other individuals as well as of society as a whole.

This startling idea, if sound, explained many things. It explained why men invariably differ; and it seemed to give a scientific support to the liberal faith that intellectual freedom and toleration are inescapably necessary for the progress of civilization. It seemed to underscore an inevitable relativity of knowledge and thought. But it also encouraged the belief that the mind, being free, is not necessarily bound by any convention, or superstition, or philosophy, but may soar away from all of them in any direction that seems good to itself.

As Berrill put it,

> Freedom begins here. The freedom to think untrammeled and to speak accordingly, the freedom for thought to soar if possible, and the freedom of the mind to be for the sake of being, in the sense that a thing of beauty is a joy forever and needs no other sanction.[13]

So far as history was concerned, this seemed to give scientific support to the idea that whereas the corpus of historical fact is something given and unchangeable, the historian's knowledge of it is, and must always be, both partial and of necessity relative to the individual historian.

[13] Berrill, *op. cit.*, 276.

This did not, however, seem of necessity to lead to complete intellectual anarchy. For there were two very powerful considerations that must inevitably operate against it. On the one hand, historians had already devised a set of canons of methodology and criticisms that would discipline and restrain within scientific bounds the individual differences among them. On the other, there did seem to exist a working consensus of historical knowledge that was constantly growing and refining itself. This consensus, until further revised and corrected, might properly be called the corpus of historical truth. It must, and would be, constantly revised by the individual talents of individual historians; but any revision might earn its way into the corpus of historical truth only by the force of incontrovertible, verifiable evidence, presented within the canons of an historically scientific method.

Historicus was now more convinced than ever that he might be justified in thinking of history as a science. A science *sui generis,* to be sure, but a science nevertheless. He felt obliged—but it was fairly easy—to reassure himself and his students that this was not the "scientism," so abhorred by F. A. Hayek[14] and others, that seeks to apply the methods of the physical sciences to human behavior. Since history's subject matter is one that is at least relatively free and unpredictable—one that "capriciously hops about,"[15] as B. F. Skinner puts it—its method must be a special one, one calculated to achieve as great a degree of accuracy as possible but never expecting mathematical accuracy or precise predictability. Perhaps this meant an attitude, rather than a method. If scientific method, after all, is nothing more than an attitude, then the most basic and most inflexible rule of historical method must always be the attitude of scientific objectivity toward historical materials.

[14] F. A. Hayek, *The Counter-Revolution of Science; Studies on the Abuse of Reason* (Glencoe, Ill., 1952), 13-16, *et passim.*
[15] Skinner, *Walden Two*, p. 214.

But was scientific objectivity possible in the study of history, after all? Historicus was convinced that relatively it was, at least in the same sense and to the same degree that it was possible to the physical scientist. Ranke had believed objectivity was possible, but every historian in the mid-twentieth century had been taught, under the influence of the climate of opinion in which he lived, that it was impossible. Scientifically speaking, there was no such thing as pure reason, if by the term was meant intelligence independent of emotion. Certainly, historically, many of the most precious monuments of civilization were the joint creations of emotion, mathematical intellect, and creative poetic fancy. Obviously, from the evidence of history, emotions and intelligence, so called, were integral and inseparable functions of the same human brain. Objectivity, in the sense of considering the corpus of historical fact with the intelligence working independently of the emotions, thus was apparently biologically inconceivable.

Yet the historian, as any other scientist, could and must remember always that his subject matter, the "what-had-happened" of history was external, or objective, to himself; and it seemed to Historicus that his whole historical method must rest upon this attitude. In this sense, objectivity *was* possible, at least in exactly the same degree that objectivity was possible to the astronomer, the physicist, the chemist, or the biologist. The human mind was a "subjective" mind, and it could not be otherwise. But it could, and must, in the consideration of external historical reality, refrain from the conscious extension of its own subjectivity to and upon the external fact. Put in simpler, more homely terms, this meant that the historian's method, whatever else it included, must include the rigorous canon that the historian must always approach his evidence as something external to himself.

This much, at least, was possible. If the astronomer could achieve a satisfactory degree of objectivity, so could the historian, and in exactly the same degree. If the historian could not do it, neither could the astronomer nor any other scientist; and to admit that the scientist could not be objective was to question the validity of all human knowledge, of whatever sort.

Historicus took great satisfaction, as a human, in his peculiarly human capability, real or imagined, to withdraw himself from the arena up into the benches—nay, up on a high hill overlooking *both* arena *and* benches—and to observe every action and every thought of every man, woman, and child who ever lived, including his contemporaries. Perhaps Toynbee was right. Perhaps the historian *was,* in the last analysis, a poet. If it were by the use of imagination that the historian, sitting on his raft floating down the flood of the moving stream of history, could, at the same time, achieve a sort of withdrawal to some high mountain from which to view the flood and all its human passengers, he might, indeed, be called a poet as well as a scientist. It was this power of psychological or imaginative withdrawal, of standing back and looking at humanity and oneself from without, that was historical objectivity. Needless to say, this scientific objectivity was the one essential and indispensable element in any valid historical method.

CRITICISM

But method for what? Given the objective reality of the corpus of historical events, what was the historian trying to do? What, indeed, did history itself—conceived as a profession dedicated to the scientific description, analysis, and interpretation of past historical events—consider to be the intellectual canons and objectives governing its investigations?

It was here, perhaps, that the historians appeared to be least in accord. For the historical writing of the mid-twentieth century had become, for many historians, less a matter of writing new historical works based upon the sources, or evidence, than the art of criticizing the work of others. And the literature of historical criticism included a variety of genera, from the lowlv book review to the brilliant critical essays of a Becker, a Geyl, a Barraclough, or a Butterfield.

Yet there seemed to be no generally accepted canons of historical criticism. Nobody had ever successfully laid down the basic principles. Every historian struck out for himself, to comment upon the work of other historians, past and present, as it occurred to him to do. Historicus did not object to this, since such behavior appeared to be consistent with the fact that all men, including historians, are biologically and otherwise intellectually different from each other. Yet it did seem desirable to seek some agreed-upon principles. After all, the fact that historians differ did not justify complete intellectual anarchy in this business of criticism. There was a consensus of historical knowledge; surely there might be a consensus of agreed-upon canons of historical criticism.

Historicus believed he might start with the axiom that man is an historically minded animal. Other animals live almost entirely in the present; they appear to be guided almost entirely, if not quite, by instincts rather than by what we have called the free intelligence. But humans have a past, and they are intensely interested in it. Why is this so? Why do so many grown men and women spend their lives burrowing in the dirty, well-nigh illegible documentary remains of five thousand or a thousand or a hundred years ago? Does man's conscious, systematic interest in his own past—a fairly recent intellectual interest that dates back hardly more than three thousand years—does this interest indicate an active aversion to the forward look? Is it a symptom of a degeneracy? Does the work of Thucydides, Polybius, Augustine, Gibbon, Ranke, Spengler, or Toynbee betray a greater interest in the past than in the future? Is it a sign of our innate human conservatism or reactionism, some nostalgic escapism that hankers after a better time in the youth of civilization? How was this peculiarly human industry to be explained?

[184]

The basic fact seemed to be that man, as no other living organism, is a learning animal. His culture is cumulative. Every generation begins, not from the beginning of cultural evolution, but where the preceding generation left off. The chances for survival of a new-born babe in the twentieth century are, perhaps, a thousand times greater than those of a child born a million years ago, because of the accumulated knowledge and inventions for his comfort and care that have been piled up for him in the meantime. The doctor who attends him, the architect who built the hospital, the scientists who provided the medicines and the instruments, the nurse, his parents, his teachers, the society in which he will live—all are what they are today, in everything except what they have themselves contributed to the great mass of human learning, because of what they have learned from those who went before. The past is infinitely important to the new-born babe in his own private struggle to survive and to achieve the good life. By the same token, the past is of infinite importance to society as a whole.

Man's culture, in other words, was cumulative, as no other animal's activity was. And it was the historian's job to make sure that the accumulation should be always available for those who would learn from it, that it should neither cease to exist nor be forgotten. The historian, as it were, was the custodian, the curator, and the interpreter of the accumulated record of human experience.

Interpretation, however, did not mean any one of several attitudes toward "interpretation" that Historicus felt sure must be ruled out of history-writing if the strict, scientific canons of historical method were rigorously observed.

He would not, for example, permit himself to fall into the trap of what was called historicism, or historical "presentism." For if the corpus of historical events is something external to the historian, and if the historian is an investigatory scientist trying to find out what the truth with regard to those events is

[185]

then his function is limited to that, and nothing more. And the historical scientist must be just as objective toward his materials as the physicist, the chemist, or the astronomer. His method of investigation was different, to be sure; his scientific attitude was the same.

It seemed to Historicus that there were surely many parts of the great objective corpus of historical reality that could not, by any stretch of the imagination, be directly related to the present. Supposing this to be so, and if the validity of history is to be judged only by its lessons for the present, why study them? What validity, measured against the standards of this "presentism," could there possibly be in the study of the history of the head-hunters of Africa or the pot-boilers of Patagonia? Must the study of history be limited to those areas of history that have a direct and demonstrable influence upon the present?

Again, it seemed to him that the history of China, the history of India, the history of the Middle East, the history of Central Africa and the history of the West flowed for millennia in parallel but separate channels. Was he to believe that all these histories, all the way back to the beginning, have some sort of formative influence upon the present in the town of Bend, Oregon? If not, are these histories to have no validity whatever, in the presentists' terms?[16]

It seemed to Historicus that the science of history could not be selective; that it must study *all* history, whether the events had any relationship to the present or not. Besides which, it seemed to him that the evidence of accumulation alone was sufficient to show that there were genuinely *new* elements in every "present" situation; therefore, it seemed to him, the present is never more than partially the outgrowth of the past; and, therefore, any attempt to show a precise and exclusive derivation of the present from the past was bound to be only

16 *Cf.* Isaiah Berlin, *Historical Inevitability* (London, 1954), or G. J. Renier, *History: Its Purpose and Method* (London, 1950).

partial, and so speculative as to preclude the possibility of arriving at accurate findings based upon *all* the evidence.

The real point was that "presentism" in any form was bound to be an unwarranted departure from historical objectivity and the canons of scientific historical method. It seemed to Historicus that a sharp line must be drawn between the historian's function of discovering the truth with regard to any event, such as the Manchu invasions or European scholasticism or the American Civil War, and the function of the publicist or the politician in putting that truth to some practical application.

This mood of "presentism" reached what was to Historicus its extreme and most profoundly erroneous form in the tendency of many of his contemporaries to sit in moral judgment upon the historical events and personalities in the history they were studying.[17]

Historicus thought he saw a thoroughly unhistorical confusion of thought in one distinguished historian's statement that

> Every historian, as we all know ... imparts his own set of moral judgments into the writing of history by the very process of inter-pretation.... an acceptance of the fact of moral responsibility does not license the historian to roam through the past ladling out individual praise and blame.... But it does mean that there are certain essential issues on which it is necessary for the historian to have a position if he is to understand the great conflicts of history.[18]

This rationalization of conscious subjective moral judgment appeared again and again in the critical writings of outstanding contemporary historians.[19] Yet, such a use of history, it seemed

---

[17] *Cf.* Isaiah Berlin, *op. cit.* Compare, also, Louis Gottschalk, "A Professor of History in a Quandary," *American Historical Review*, LIX, 277-278, or Kenneth Stampp, *The Peculiar Institution* (New York, 1956), page vii.

[18] Arthur Meier Schlesinger, Jr., "The Causes of the Civil War," *Partisan Review*, XVI, 978-979.

[19] See, for example, Herbert Butterfield, *Man on His Past* (Cambridge, 1955); Isaiah Berlin, *op. cit.*; Peter Geyl, *Debates with Historians* (Groningen, 1955).

to Historicus, rested upon the assumption of some moral absolute, or set of absolutes, that governs, or should govern, the behavior of all men at all times and in all places. Furthermore, it seemed to assume that the historian could be absolutely sure his own moral convictions conformed to the absolute and that those of Nero, or Tamurlane, or Adolf Hitler, say, did not.

Historicus could accept neither of these assumptions. His reading of history, with its record of a vast variety of moral practices and ideas—often, as between one civilization and another directly contradictory to each other—convinced him that far from demonstrating, or even suggesting, the existence of an absolute morality among men, the record is a stark, irrevocable, and overwhelming demonstration of the exact opposite.

Historicus was convinced that it is not the historian's job to apportion moral responsibility. Aside from the apparent intellectual arrogance and moral conceit implied, it seemed that the record of history itself shows irrefutably that the canons of morality are highly relative, from time to time and from place to place. Idolatry, suttee, the Inquisition of the Feudal Era, and a belief in the persecution of witches have all been regarded as highly moral in certain times and places and by millions upon millions of human beings.

Was the worship of Mylitta, the Great Mother, with its temple prostitutes, immoral? It was practiced by thousands of men for hundreds of years. Was the practice of polygyny immoral? It was practiced by millions of men through thousands of years; it is still practiced. As Will Rogers said, "We have polygyny, only it ain't legal." Upon what basis of fact or logic can the historian proclaim that all those billions of practicers of polygyny were guilty of immorality? Furthermore, if the historian accepted the biologist's proposition that no two men think alike, then they would be bound to differ morally, also; and if this were so, it would be biologically unthinkable for one little human being to decide for the rest of the human race, past, present, and future, what might be good for them—or simply what was the good.

Historicus could only conclude that moral judgment upon his subject matter on the part of the historian was utterly irrelevant to the historian's true vocation. What is the validity, for the student of history today, of the moral pontifications of Carlyle or Macaulay? He finds them quaintly amusing; they have absolutely no validity as history.

But the tendency among historians in the middle of the twentieth century to moralize upon their materials seemed to Historicus to invite scrutiny for another reason. For it appeared to him to come dangerously close to being just another manifestation of the religious and moral revival of the mid-twentieth century, which appeared to him to be one of the facets of the current mood of conservatism and intellectual loss of nerve in all the departments of life. If this were so—if it were, really, merely the historian's way of participating in the great religious and moral revival that characterized the social moods of his time—then it did seem to be a frightening confirmation of the bold, history-destroying tenet of the behavioralists that all thinking, including historical thinking, is social thinking. In this light, the historian's moral judgment upon history became his generation's moral judgment, merely one of the voices of his society and, like all such social judgments, "full of sound and fury, signifying nothing," except to the society that accepts it.

In the seventeenth century Increase Mather, student of comets, felt sure the comet was a sign of God's anger at New England; in the eighteenth, Thomas Prince, student of earthquakes, severely chided Professor John Winthrop for his scientific objectivity in describing the earthquake of 1755. Yet since that time the astronomers and the geologists have learned that at least a high degree of objectivity is not only possible but even imperatively necessary if those sciences are to continue to advance. Since the mass of historical fact is external to the historical observer, Historicus asked why the same sort of progress toward objectivity should not be made by the historians. It seemed to him that if the historians appeared to be in danger of becoming a disappearing race[20] it might well be because they had failed to achieve a reasonable degree of objectivity, and, on the other hand, had permitted themselves to indulge in a lot of moralizing that could have little challenge or validity for anybody in the historian's own generation except the moralizer himself, and probably none whatever for the students of history in succeeding generations.

Of course, in the sense that all knowledge, all understanding, is ultimately moral, or ethical, since understanding is a basic factor in intelligent or moral decisions, history does, inevitably, have its moral value. Furthermore, while the historian himself is no moral propagandist and while he should eschew as the plague the temptation to sit in moral judgment upon his material, if the knowledge and the understanding of men he reveals is taken by preachers, politicians, or humane societies as intellectual bases upon which to construct institutions or laws or customs calculated to increase the sum total of human happiness, then the study of history does, indeed, if indirectly, have a highly moral outcome. The historian merely remembers he is not, *qua* historian, a supporter of moral causes. He is a scientist; his attitude must be that of a scientist.

By a similar line of reasoning, Historicus was led to repudiate the related ideas of causality and inevitability in history. As he studied the facts in the field of history in which he did his own research, he could discover no convincing evidence that one event or series of events ever caused or made inevitable, exactly as it happened, another event or series of events.

The only identifiable "cause" of historical events appeared to be man. And if man's intelligence is free, even in the slightest conceivable degree, his action in response to any given event

[20] *Cf.* Whyte, *The Organization Man,* chap. 2.

or influence is likely to be the result of a relatively free choice of one of many possible actions. He has the faculty of choosing among these possible paths, and he does choose; he is not compelled to make any particular choice. His choice is made at the prompting of one or more "motives," conscious or unconscious; but motivation is hardly to be equated with causation; and who is to determine the cause of a given set of motives in a man, even if all the motives could be known?

What, for example, was the "cause" that made "inevitable" the settlement of Virginia by Englishmen? The only possible answer is "Englishmen." Why were some Englishmen interested and others not? And why should there have been such a wide difference of motivation among those who did go? Why should Virginia not have been settled by Spaniards, or Frenchmen, or Dutchmen? There was no identifiable "cause" for these facts, and the settlement by Englishmen, in that precise pattern, was surely not inevitable. It is historically impossible to find a "cause" for this event—or any other in history—or to say that it was inevitable. Contributing factors there were, yes; limitations upon choice, certainly; but determinism in any direct sense, no.

What is the cause of a river? Is it the force of gravity? Or is it meteorological conditions that result in rainfall? Or is it the geological conformation of the earth? Or is it the chemistry of water? Or is it a combination of all these? Certainly no one of these can be singled out as *the* cause.

History is like that. There is no single identifiable cause of any event or course of events. Nor is it possible to identify all the multiplicity of causal influences possibly contributing to bringing an event to pass. An event may be said to be an outgrowth of many things, like the fruit that appears on a chestnut tree; that any one, or any combination of many *caused* it, it is impossible to say. History *grows,* like a tree, or *flows,* like a river; it seemed to Historicus that it was utterly futile to seek for causation in history, except, perhaps, for the individual reactions of individual men; but to speak of even individual motivation as historical causation was so superficial as to be meaningless.

Similarly, but in certain ways by contrast, Historicus found it necessary to dismiss the idea of inevitability. Thus, again, if history is a river flowing down the channels and valleys of time, it is, nevertheless, possible to direct it, and change its course by the use of human intelligence. By their intelligence men have dammed rivers, or redirected them, and they have converted the power of the flowing water into the power to light their cities and turn the wheels of their mills. And individual men— Buddha, Confucius, Aristotle, Jesus, Einstein—have given direction to, and drawn power from, the river that is history. Nothing is inevitable in history except the flow of history itself, which will continue as long as human beings populate the globe. The flow will continue, but the past itself demonstrates unquestionably that men, by taking thought, may control the direction of its flow and draw from it power and inspiration for the lighting of the darkest areas of their living.

This means, of course, that men, as relatively free animals, are also *responsible,* within certain natural limits, for their own history. It is difficult to imagine a great lumber industry flourishing in the Mojave Desert, for example, or the growing of date-palms on the shores of Hudson Bay. Yet within the limitations provided by geography and the nature of man himself, men do decide what they will or will not do. The range of choice is always limited; but men do choose.

Finally, Historicus could not follow either Toynbee or Niebuhr or Augustine of Hippo in the assumption that history reveals a plan for human destiny emanating from the mind of some supernatural being. As a part of their search for ideas that might explain to them phenomena that they otherwise could not explain, or to satisfy subjective desires for an escape from the problems of reality of which they were conscious, men, to be sure, had attributed these phenomena to supernatural sources. In India the attribution took one form, in China another, in Egypt another, among the American Indians another, in ancient Greece another. And literally billions of men have lived upon the basis of the assumption that these attributions were true. Yet in all the corpus of historical fact Historicus could not find the slightest shred of verifiable evidence that some supernatural entity did, actually, at some time or another exercise some influence upon the affairs of men.

Both logic and the nature of the historical evidence thus led him to reject *as a matter of history* the idea of supernatural causation. The historian, as the astronomer, may, as a person and out of subjective reasons or emotions that seem satisfying to him, assume, upon the basis of a subjective faith alone, that some supernatural entity does exist and that it does influence the course of history. As an historical scientist, however, he must not go beyond his evidence, any more than the astronomer or the physicist may do so.

Thus any belief in a supernatural reality, which must be based upon faith alone, and not evidence, Historicus had to rule out of the historian's province. He simply found that there is no evidence for it as a factor in history; and he emerged from this meditation in complete agreement with the distinguished theologian Karl Lowith that

> In the Christian view the history of salvation is no longer bound up with a particular nation but is internationalized because it is individualized. In Christianity the history of salvation is related to the salvation of each single soul, regardless of racial, social, and political status, and the contribution of the nations to the Kingdom of God is measured by the number of the elect, not by any corporate achievement or failure. From this it follows that the historical destiny of Christian peoples is no possible subject of a specifically Christian interpretation of political history.[21]

21 Karl Lowith, *Meaning in History* (Chicago, 1949), 193, 195.

Max Savelle

History, for Historicus, was a science that studies and explains the evidence of the past. Theology, as morality, was quite another matter.

Very well. If these were the negative canons of historical criticism, what were the positive ones? If one subtracted from history all "presentism," moral judgment, causality, inevitability, and the influence of the supernatural, what had one left?

Historicus could only reply, the science of history. By that he meant the formulation, on the basis of the objective evidence, of some fragments of historical truth and understanding. The historian's job, as a discoverer and describer of the facts, is an extremely important one in civilization, which always rests in very large part, though not entirely, upon the learning of the past. But his importance is very great, also, as a formulator of knowledge and understanding for its own sake. It is difficult to imagine any direct utility or moral lesson to be learned from understanding the Mayan calendar, for example, or the social customs of the ancient Australian bushmen; but there is a profound satisfaction, nevertheless, in knowing them. Furthermore, such fragments of knowledge—added to many others, of course—do, it appeared, provide a foundation for an understanding of the basic nature of human behavior everywhere.

History, as a science, stood on its own feet. It was not one of the social sciences, although it did study the history of human society; it was not a behavioral science, although it was an objective study of human behavior in the past. Its methodology was different from the methodology of every other branch of human learning; and it was concerned, as no other science, with the dynamics of the historical process, the process of the cumulative enrichment of human experience and human culture.

One question remained: in what way, if any, could the historian be said to be a creative writer, a builder, an artist, a contributor to the culture-complex upon which future civilization will rest? If he could build no Taj Mahal, write no Shakespearean sonnet, and launch no earth satellite, what could he do of a positive sort? Bound as he was by his evidence, in what ways could the historian express an impulse, if he had any, to be *creative?*

The author, the poet, the architect, the philosopher, the atomic scientists—these were creative artists or inventors. Was the study of history inevitably backward-looking? Could the historian never think for himself as a creative, forward-looking thinker?

As Historicus pondered this question, his path long remained unclear. Yet he was not content, and could never be, to stop here, to face backward, forever to concentrate upon the contemplation of the hills and valleys behind him that he, with all mankind, had hitherto traversed. Even if he did no more than recreate the past with such great accuracy and art as to inform and inspire his readers, the historian was an artist as well as a scientist. But at his best, the historian might create a whole philosophy, based upon the historical evidence, of the nature of man and his place in the universe. And other men, reading it, might be led to ponder the more, and the more perfectly to understand, their own relationship to the cosmos.

PHILOSOPHY

The highest reach of history, then, was the level at which it became a philosophy, an explanation of the nature of man and of man's place in the world. When the historian could achieve such a philosophy of man's existence he became, in truth, a creative thinker and writer, creating his systems of thought not out of the pure flights of ratiocination or of fantasy out of which poetry is born, but, rather, out of the solid factual evidence testifying to the things that had actually happened in the course of human cultural evolution.

Historicus had been born and reared in the age when man learned that the basic stuff of matter is electronic energy and had invented ways and means of controlling the basic processes of matter to his own ends. Though in his youth strongly conditioned by a quasi-fundamentalist religious explanation of the nature of things, it was, nevertheless, probably not unnatural that Historicus had finally arrived at a full acceptance of the scientific explanation of the nature of reality.

A philosophy of history resting upon this explanation of existence thus subsumed, first, a material universe of electronic matter in which life, including human life, was a manifestation of one of the complexes of the activities of matter. Man, one of the forms of life, had evolved biologically to the point where his brain was a far more effective instrument in the struggle to survive than that of any other animal; it was by the use of this instrument that man had come to dominate the earth and to make almost all other forms of life obsolete except insofar as he might choose to perpetuate them because they were useful to him.

In the course of man's evolution the human brain had developed certain functional mechanisms which, although the same or analogous mechanisms had appeared in other animals, were in him so far refined and specialized as to present the faculties of memory, of free intelligent choice, and of creative imagination. *Homo sapiens,* at least, was now in large measure capable of directing his own destiny; and recorded history was the story of how, for the past ten thousand years, he had done it.

But every individual human mind or intelligence is biologically different from every other; and the use of mind or intelligence in the struggle to survive becomes a matter of the exercise of both individual minds and an exchange of ideas or consensus called the "group mind" (or, more accurately, "opinion"), the latter of which expresses itself through what has been called a "consensus" of a society or group at a given time or place. Every historic event was the product of the effort of individual human animals, or groups of them, to achieve some end that was thought

[196]

to be described in this struggle. But the irrational biological emotions were often more powerful than the rational intelligence; often the rational intelligence was employed to achieve an irrational end. The result was a course of human history filled with actions that were often cruel, irrational, intolerant, mystical, or even suicidal. The human intelligence, if free to choose its way, was also free, from the point of view of its own long-term benefit, to err.

History seemed to show that this mechanism, the human mind, while it was the most significant biological mechanism yet evolved on this earth, was still a highly undependable, highly temperamental, and highly imperfect instrument. It seemed to Historicus, nevertheless, that if the chief difference between humans and all other animals was that man had a history, the reason why this difference existed was that man first had a free, inquiring mind; and all history became, for Historicus, simply the record of the human mind, imperfect as it was, and more often than not in the service of the emotions, at work.

Where primitive emotion has been the chief driving force, men have struggled not only with the other animals and with the forces of nature, but, also, with each other. Yet gradually and in a multiplicity of forms, the force of intelligence or ideas has tended to replace the savage survival values of violence and brute force with the more effective values of religion, of philosophy, of the arts, and above all and most recently, of science.

Indeed, it appeared to be science, an intellectual phenomenon, which might at last have instructed man as to the true nature of the universe and of himself in it. For he had not only learned the nature of the basic structure of matter; he had also achieved a technique of manipulation of it that had opened, it might be, the most spectacular era, thus far, in man's history; that is, if he should prove to be sufficiently intelligent to avoid using this new-found mental power to destroy himself.

The history of human civilization as distinguished from sheer

[197]

animal savagery, thus, in the last analysis, did appear to be the history of the human mind at work; and Historicus was inclined to agree with Collingwood at least insofar as to recognize that every significant historical event was first preceded by an idea.

Historicus was not a determinist or an advocate of "scientism" in history. History was a "science-that-is-also-an-art," to be sure, but its subject matter was a creature that "capriciously hops about." Since the mind of the creature is in some small measure free, he is in that measure independent of the natural laws of instinct and predictability that govern the behavior of the lower animals. Since he has a certain freedom of choice, in any instance, his behavior, though the behavior of masses of men may be measured and extrapolated statistically, may never, in specific individual cases, be accurately predicted or controlled. This was a sort of principle of human "indeterminacy."

Such a philosophy of history is purely naturalistic and entirely humanistic. As for meaning in history, Historicus could find none, except, possibly, the meaning inherent in the universal fact of the struggle to survive and find the good life. As a naturalist in his philosophy, he could see, for example, no evidence of, or necessity for a cyclical interpretation of history. By the appearances, it did seem to be true that civilizations rose and declined, if by that was meant that they passed through alternate periods of greater and lesser creative activity. But it seemed to him that the appearance gave a false impression. For it could not be denied that Egyptian civilization was continuous, from before the fifth millennium B.C. to beyond the end of the second millennium A.D., however much it fluctuated in culture, religion, or political forms. Indian civilization passed through a series of phases, as it were; but it remained the same civilization. Chinese civilization, similarly, alternated between periods of intensely creative intellectual, cultural, economic, and political activity and periods of relative quietness or stagnation. It seemed to Historicus that the evidence—all the evidence—showed that the history of any given civilization is rectilinear, not cyclical.

It seemed to Historicus, then, that the explanation of human history that most nearly answered all the questions was that which saw the human animal as nothing more nor less than that one of the products of biological evolution which had—happily for him but unhappily for all other living creatures on the globe—evolved a biological mechanism, called by him the brain, or intelligence, to a degree of effectiveness that gave him a distinct advantage over all his rivals in the struggle for survival.

That was not to say, of course, that this mechanism always worked well, or even for this animal's own good. Coupled as it was, also, with the highly irrational drives and emotions over which the intelligence had little or no control, and the notorious tendency of the animal to react first and to think afterward, it appeared to Historicus that it was now easy to understand why the history of the civilizations built by this curious blob of protoplasm was so studded with behavior which, in the terms of the animal's own self-interest, could only be described as asinine.

And yet, even while recognizing the high percentage of asininity in human behavior, Historicus could not escape a sense of exhilaration that it was nevertheless this same human intelligence that, whether in the service of irrational emotions or in that of pure, objective knowledge, had written the Vedas, the Analects, the Dialogues of Plato, the Divine Comedy, or the plays of Shakespeare; it had built the Taj Mahal, the Parthenon, the Cathedral at Chartres, and Grand Coulee Dam; above all, it had discovered the workings of the universe and the innermost secrets of the ultimate structure of matter, and had turned this knowledge to the service of human beings in their struggle to survive and find the good life.

Historicus wondered a little whether the animal would meet the final test of intelligence and use his terrifying knowledge for the continuing purposes of survival, or whether his persistent and apparently never-diminishing quotient of imbecility—which some had dignified by calling it original sin—would lead him to the use of this ultimate control over matter to clear the earth of the human encumbrance altogether so it could return to its original natural and non-human-infested state. But this speculation was but a passing shadow. Even if the animal used its knowledge and control of the atom to commit a genuine, world-wide race suicide, the achievement of the human mind involved was still unshakeably magnificent, and Historicus could only feel happy that he was a human, and not, say, a tomcat or a sea urchin.

No, he could find no meaning in history, and he could agree wholeheartedly with Herbert J. Muller that

> History has no meaning, in the sense of a clear pattern or determinate plot; but it is not simply meaningless or pointless. It has no certain meaning because man is free to give it various possible meanings. . . .
>
> Among the possible "meanings" of history . . . the most significant is the growth of this power of self-determination, or freedom to make history. I assume that for interpreting the past and choosing a future we must begin with a full acknowledgment of the claims of reason: a humble reason that makes no claim to finality or metaphysical certitude, because such claims cannot be rationally substantiated, and that recognizes its finiteness and fallibility; a proud reason that nevertheless maintains its authority as the final judge of all claims to truth, insisting that its tested knowledge is no less real and reliable because it is not a knowledge of [some] ultimate [metaphysical] reality, and that only by a further exercise of reason can its limitations and its fallacies be clearly discerned.[22]

CONCLUSION

At this point Historicus passed the tree-line on his mountain and emerged into the free, clear, unimpeded vision of the range upon range of human reality that lay stretched out before him. Breathtaking in its vastness and its complexity, if admittedly

[22] Herbert J. Muller, *The Uses of the Past* (New York, 1952), 73-74.

still only a partial view of the whole scene, could his mind but encompass it, the panorama of the human past lay, real and observable, before him. All the discrepancies seemed to fall into place; all the problems appeared, at last, to be susceptible of workable, logical, and honest solutions.

The study of history seemed to show that it was the nature of man, among animals, to be relatively free; it was his destiny to make his own destiny. History, with all its vicissitudes, was the record of how he had done it. But the record was cumulative, and man was a learning animal who passed on what he had learned from generation to generation.

The historian, the scientist-who-is-also-an-artist, was the discoverer, the analyzer, the preserver, and the transmitter of the record. As a scientist he was bound by the discipline of his critical rules of evidence. But as an individual mind and creative philosopher he "painted the thing as he saw it," freely and honestly on the basis of the evidence.

If history had any didactic value at all it lay in the value of teaching men their own capabilities—that they do make their own destiny, that they are free, within limitations, to shape it as they will, and that they are responsible for the result.

Was this the "Holy Wisdom" Historicus had been seeking? It was, in the sense that the realization of freedom and responsibility is wisdom. It was not, in the sense that freedom was only the necessary condition for the achievement of further wisdom. Wisdom itself, whether of the individual or the group, was only relative, and could never be perfect or absolute.

This meant that the Quest was not ended. Nor could it ever be. The appetite for Wisdom "grew by what it fed on"; the quest for it could never have an end.

BIBLIOGRAPHY

BOOKS

George Morgan, Colony Builder. New York: Columbia University Press, 1932.

The Diplomatic History of the Canadian Boundary, 1749-1793. New Haven, Conn.: Yale University Press, 1940.

Foundations of American Civilization. New York: Henry Holt & Co., 1942. (Revised with Robert Middlekauf as, *A History of Colonial America.* New York: Holt, Rinehart & Winston, 1964.)

Seeds of Liberty. New York: Alfred A. Knopf, Inc., 1948. (Republished by University of Washington Press, both hardback and paperback, in 1965.)

This Is My America: Pauline Dworzek and the Dworzek and Lorber Families. Stanford, Calif.: Stanford University Press, 1948.

The United States: Colonial Period (Part II, Vol. 4, of *Programa de historia de América,* edited by S. Zavala). Mexico, D.F.: Pan-American Institute of Geography and History, 1953. (An English abridgement by Max Savelle was published in 1961, along with a Spanish translation of the new abridgement by Antonio Alatorre.)

A History of World Civilization (general editor and contributor). 2 vols. New York: Henry Holt & Co., 1957. (A 4-volume

Spanish translation was published by Marín in Barcelona in 1959.)

A Short History of American Civilization (with the assistance of Tremaine McDowell). New York: The Dryden Press, 1957. (A Spanish translation was published in 1961 by Gredos in Madrid.)

The Colonial Origins of American Thought. New York: Van Nostrand (Anvil Books), 1964.

ARTICLES AND PAMPHLETS

"Colonial Origins of American Diplomatic Principles," *Pacific Historical Review,* III (September, 1934), 334-50.

"George Morgan," in *Dictionary of American Biography,* XIII (1934), 169-70.

"New European Alignments. Summary of Round Tables" (as general chairman), *Proceeedings of the Institute of World Affairs,* XIV (December, 1936), 71-78.

"What Is a Liberal Education?" *School and Society,* XLVIII (October, 1938), 558-61. (Republished in *Our Changing World,* by S. F. Anderson, *et al.* New York: Harper & Brothers, 1939. Pp. 189-94.)

"Diplomatic Preliminaries of the Seven Years War in America," *The Canadian Historical Review,* XX (March, 1939), 17-39.

"The American Balance of Power and European Diplomacy, 1713-1778," in *The Era of the American Revolution,* edited by R. B. Morris. New York: Columbia University Press, 1939. Pp. 140-69. (Republished in paperback by Harper and Row, 1965.)

"New Madrid, Missouri," "Paris, The Treaty of (1763)," "Ryswick, The Peace of (1697)," in *Dictionary of American History,* edited by J. T. Adams and R. V. Coleman. 2nd rev. ed.; New York: Charles Scribner's Sons, 1940. Vol. IV, pp. 106, 216, 512.

"Spanish Foundations of Hemispheric Solidarity," and "European Dangers to Hemispheric Co-operation" (as chairman), *Proceedings of the Institute of World Affairs,* XVIII (December, 1940), 133-37, 177-80.

"History and the World Revolution," *School and Society,* LVII (January, 1943), 61-64.

"History and Citizenship in a Democracy," *The Eleusis of Chi Omega,* XLV (May, 1943), 224-37.

"The Appearance of an American Attitude Toward External Affairs, 1750-1775," *American Historical Review,* LII (July 1947), 655-66. (Republished in *The Shaping of American Diplomacy,* edited by W. A. Williams. Chicago: Rand McNally & Co., 1956. Pp. 13-21.)

"The Imperial School of American Colonial Historians," *Indiana Magazine of History,* XLV (June, 1949), 123-34.

"Road to Revolution," in *Problems in American History,* edited by R. W. Leopold and A. S. Link. New York: Prentice-Hall, Inc., 1952. Pp. 44-87. (Republished in 2nd ed.; Englewood Cliffs, N.J.: Prentice-Hall, Inc., 1957. Pp. 27-70.)

Roger Williams, Dissenter and Democrat (radio broadcast, published separately). New York: Broadcast Music, Inc., 1954.

Apuntes sobre los orígenes de la cultura en Norteamérica (address delivered at the Casa Americana, Madrid, Spain, published separately). Madrid: U. S. Embassy, 1954.

"History, Photography, and the Library," *Library Journal,* LX (Nov. 15, 1955), 873-77.

"The Teacher and Intellectual Freedom in the United States," *Pacific Spectator,* X (Winter, 1956), 15-26.

"Roger Williams, A Minority of One," in *The American Story; The Age of Exploration to the Age of the Atom,* edited by E. S. Miers. Great Neck, N.Y.: Channel Press, 1956. Pp. 50-55.

"Aims in College Teaching and Learning," *Improving College and University Teaching,* V (Winter, 1957), 9-15.

"Democratic Government of the State University—A Proposal," *American Association of University Professors Bulletin,* XLIII (June, 1957), 323-28.

Bibliography

"The Forty-Ninth Degree of North Latitude as an International Boundary, 1719: The Origin of an Idea," *Canadian Historical Review*, XXXVII (September, 1957), 183-201.

"Is Liberalism Dead?" *The Historian*, XX (November, 1957), 3-23.

"El Curso de las Ideas Liberales en los Estados Unidos de América hasta fines del Siglo XIX" and "El Liberalismo en los Estados Unidos durante el Siglo XX," in *El Liberalismo y la reforma en México*, by H. Medina, *et al.* Mexico City: Universidad Nacional, 1957. Pp. 151-53, 155-77.

"Los Dominios Ingleses en el Siglo XVII" and "Los Dominios Ingleses en el Siglo XVIII," in *Historia Americana*, edited by A. Vinardell. 4 vols. Buenos Aires: Lasserre, 1957.

"Historian's Progress or The Quest for Sancta Sophia," *Pacific Historical Review*, XXVII (February, 1958), 1-26.

"Summary of Conference on Religion" (with Doctor J. Malagon), *The Americas*, XIV (April, 1958), 524-37.

"America, in the New, World-wide Relationships," *Cahiers d'Histoire Mondiale*, IV (Part 3, 1958), 753-59. (A condensation in English of a larger work in Spanish by S. Zavala.)

Cotton Mather (radio broadcast, published separately). New York: Broadcast Music, Inc., 1958. (Republished in *The Unforgettable Americans*, edited by J. A. Garraty. Great Neck, N.Y.: Channel Press, 1960. Pp. 32-35.)

"La Historia de las Ideas en los Estados Unidos," *Revista de Historia de las Ideas*, I (November, 1959), pp. 177-89.

"The Cultivation of the Proud Mind of Man," *The Biologist*, XLII (December, 1959), 1-4.

"The Functions of History in the Age of Science," *The Historian*, XXII (August, 1960), 347-60. (Published in Spanish in *Atlántico*, XVII (1960), 5-22.)

"Prolegomena to a History of Liberalism in Eighteenth-Century Anglo-America," *Bucknell Review*, IX (December, 1960), 224-46.

"Nationalism and Other Loyalties in the American Revolution," *American Historical Review*, LXVII (July, 1962), 901-23. (Re-

Bibliography

published in *The Dynamics of Nationalism: Readings in Its Meaning and Development,* edited by L. L. Snyder. Princeton, N.J.: Van Nostrand Press, 1964. Pp. 254-57.)

"El espíritu de la independencia americana," in *Tres lecciones inaugurales.* Santiago, Chile: Centro de investigaciones de historia americana of the University of Chile, 1963.

"Benjamin Franklin and American Liberalism," *Western Humanities Review,* XVIII (Summer, 1964), 197-209.

"Thanksgiving Day," in *Holidays, Days of Significance for All America,* edited by T. N. Dupuy. New York: Franklin Watts, Inc., 1965. Pp. 133-37.

REVIEWS

Uribe, A. J. *Colombia y los Estados Unidos de America. Hispanic American Historical Review,* XIII (May, 1933), 213-15.

Foreman, G. *The Adventures of James Collier, First Collector of the Port of San Francisco. Pacific Historical Review,* VI (December, 1937), 384-85.

Bemis, S. F. *A Diplomatic History of the United States. Political Science Quarterly,* LIII (March, 1938), 146-48.

Pares, R. *War and Trade in the West Indies, 1739-1763. Hispanic American Historical Review,* XVIII (November, 1938), 535-38.

Prestage, E. *Portugal and the War of the Spanish Succession. American Historical Review,* XLV (October, 1939), 190.

Barzun, J. *Human Freedom. Frontiers of Democracy,* VI (December 15, 1939), 91.

Neurath, O. *Modern Man in the Making. Frontiers of Democracy,* VI (March 15, 1940), 186-89.

Pares, R. *Colonial Blockade and Neutral Rights, 1739-1763. Hispanic American Historical Review,* XX (May, 1940), 254-56.

Gipson, L. H. *The British Empire Before the American Revolution* (Vol. IV, *Zones of International Friction: North America, South of the Great Lakes Region, 1748-1754*). *American Historical Review,* XLV (July, 1940), 890-92.

Dorn, W. *Competition for Empire. Hispanic American Historical Review,* XX (November, 1940), 591-93.

Bibliography

Hammond, O. G. (ed.). *Letters and Papers of Major-General John Sullivan, Continental Army* (Vol. III, 1779-1795). *New England Quarterly*, XIII (December, 1940), 739-41.

Spector, M. M. *The American Department of the British Government, 1768-1782. New England Quarterly*, XIII (December, 1940), 741-42.

Koontz, L. H. *Robert Dinwiddie. American Historical Review*, XLVII (January, 1942), 347-48.

Ireland, G. *Boundaries, Possessions and Conflicts in Central and North America and the Caribbean. Political Science Quarterly*, LVII (June, 1942), 311-12.

Stevens, S. K., and D. H. Kent (eds.). *The Papers of Colonel Henry Bouquet* (Series 21631-32, 21634, 21643-46, 21652-54). And Stevens, S. K., and D. H. Kent (eds.). *Wilderness Chronicles of Northwestern Pennsylvania. Canadian Historical Review*, XXIII (June, 1942), 203-4.

Caldwell, N. W. *The French in the Mississippi Valley, 1740-1750. Pennsylvania Magazine of History and Biography*, LXVI (October, 1942), 488-89.

Conn, S. *Gibraltar in British Diplomacy in the Eighteenth Century. Hispanic American Historical Review*, XXIII (May, 1943), 332-34.

Gipson, L. H. *The British Empire Before the American Revolution* (Vol. V, *Zones of International Friction: The Great Lakes Frontier, Canada, The West Indies, India, 1748-1754*). *Political Science Quarterly*, LVIII (June, 1943), 288-90.

Long, M. H. *A History of the Canadian People. American Historical Review*, XLIX (October, 1943), 132-33.

Johnson, C. *British West Florida, 1763-1783. Hispanic American Historical Review*, XXIII (November, 1943), 739-40.

Brenan, G. *The Spanish Labyrinth. Political Science Quarterly*, LIX (March, 1944), 128-29.

Binkley, W. E. *American Political Parties. Pacific Historical Review*, XIII (June, 1944), 200-201.

Stevens, S. K., and D. H. Kent (eds.). *The Papers of Colonel Henry Bouquet* (Series 21647-48, Parts 1-2; 21649, Parts 1-2;

Bibliography

21650, Parts 1-2; 21651 and 21655). *Canadian Historical Review,* XXV (June, 1944), 204-5.

Burckhardt, J. *Force and Freedom: Reflections on History. Journal of the History of Ideas,* V (June, 1944), 374-76.

Greene, E. B. *The Revolutionary Generation, 1763-1790. Canadian Historical Review,* XXV (December, 1944), 439-40.

Adams, J. T. *et al. Album of American History* (Vol. I, *Colonial Period*). *American Historical Review,* L (January, 1945), 341-43.

"The Flight from Reason." Review article of E. Kahler, *Man the Measure,* and L. Mumford, *Condition of Man. Journal of Modern History,* XVII (June, 1945), 153-62.

Wriston, H. M. *Strategy of Peace. Pacific Historical Review,* XIV (September, 1945), 373-75.

Brebner, J. B. *North Atlantic Triangle. Pacific Historical Review,* XV (December, 1946), 443-44.

Gipson, L. H. *The British Empire Before the American Revolution* (Vol. VI, *The Great War for the Empire: The Years of Defeat, 1754-1757*). *American Historical Review,* LII (January, 1947), 331-34.

Craven, A., and W. Johnson. *United States: Experiment in Democracy. Annals of the American Academy of Political and Social Science,* CCLVI (March, 1948), 181-83.

Howard, C. N. *The British Development of West Florida, 1763-1769. Mississippi Valley Historical Review,* XXXIV (March, 1948), 677-78.

Smith, A. E. *Colonists in Bondage. Annals of the American Academy of Political and Social Science,* CCLIX (September, 1948), 160-61.

Coleman, R. V. *The First Frontier. Mississippi Valley Historical Review,* XXXV (March, 1949), 677-78.

Wright, L. B. *The Atlantic Frontier. Journal of Modern History,* XXI (March, 1949), 89-90.

Wertenbaker, T. J. *The Puritan Oligarchy. Journal of Modern History,* XXI (September, 1949), 241-43.

Bibliography

Peattie, R. (ed.). *The Cascades. Pacific Historical Review,* XIX (November, 1950), 440-41.

Gottschalk, L. *Lafayette between the American and the French Revolution (1783-1789). Mississippi Valley Historical Review,* XXXVII (December, 1950), 520-23.

Kraus, M. *The Atlantic Civilization: Eighteenth Century Origins. Political Science Quarterly,* LXV (December, 1950), 626-28.

Wish, Harvey. *Society and Thought in Early America* (Vol. I). *American Historical Review,* LVI (July, 1951), 901-2.

Baym, M. I. *The French Education of Henry Adams. Mississippi Valley Historical Review,* XXXVIII (March, 1952), 724-26.

Jensen, M. (ed.). *Regionalism in America. Pacific Historical Review,* XXI (November, 1952), 381-85.

Mays, D. J. *Edmund Pendleton, 1721-1803: A Biography* (Vols. I-II). *Mississippi Valley Historical Review,* XL (June, 1953), 118-21.

Morison, S. E. *By Land and By Sea. Inter-American Review of Bibliography,* IV (January-March, 1954), 103-4.

Morgan, E. S., and H. M. *The Stamp Act Crisis. Annals of the American Academy of Political and Social Science,* CCXCII (March, 1954), 159-60.

Stourzh, G. *Benjamin Franklin and American Foreign Policy. Journal of Modern History,* XXVII (June, 1955), 183-84.

Notestein, W. *The English People on the Eve of Colonization, 1603-1630. William and Mary Quarterly,* 3rd Series, XII (July, 1955), 500-501.

"The Philosophy of the General: Toynbee Versus the Naturalists." Review article of A. J. Toynbee, *Study of History* (Vols. I-X). *Pacific Historical Review,* XXV (February, 1956), 55-67.

Shipton, C. K. *Sibley's Harvard Graduates* (Vol. IX, *Biographical Sketches of Those Who Attended Harvard College in the Classes 1731-1735, with Bibliographical and Other Notes*). *Mississippi Valley Historical Review,* XLIII (March, 1957), 665-66.

Bibliography

Morgan, E. S. *The Birth of the Republic, 1763-1789*. *William and Mary Quarterly*, 3rd Series, XIV (October, 1957), 608-18.

Gipson, L. H. *The British Empire Before the American Revolution* (Vol. IX, *The Triumphant Empire: New Responsibilities Within the Enlarged Empire, 1763-1766*). *Historian*, XX (November, 1957), 105-6.

Burlingame, R. *The American Conscience*. *Political Science Quarterly*, LXXII (December, 1957), 630-31.

"The Mexican Constitution of 1857." Review article of D. C. Villegas, *La Constitución de 1857 y sus críticos*. *Inter-American Review of Bibliography*, VIII (January-March, 1958), 31-34.

Schlesinger, A. M. *Prelude to Independence*. *Saturday Review*, XLI (Feb. 8, 1958), 19-20.

Wright, L. B. *The Cultural Life of the American Colonies*. *New England Quarterly*, XXXI (March, 1958), 103-5.

Kohn, H. *American Nationalism—An Interpretative Essay*. *American Historical Review*, LXIII (April, 1958), 692-93.

Burns, E. M. *The American Idea of Mission: Concepts of National Purpose and Destiny*. *American Historical Review*, LXIII (July, 1958), 994-95.

"Of Fish and the River." Review article of A. Netboy, *Salmon of the Pacific Northwest: Fish vs. Dams*. *Pacific Northwest Quarterly*, L (January, 1959), 26-27.

"The Frontier; A Symposium." Review article of W. D. Wyman and C. B. Kroeber (eds.), *The Frontier in Perspective*. *Inter-American Review of Bibliography*, IX (April-June, 1959), 151-56 (in two parts, pp. 151-53 by Max Savelle, and pp. 154-56 by Marta M. de Sánchez-Albornoz).

Alden, J. R. *The South in the Revolution*. *Canadian Historical Review*, XL (June, 1959), 169-70.

Boorstin, D. J. *The Americans: The Colonial Experience*. *Political Science Quarterly*, LXXIV (June, 1959), 304-6.

Mendoza, A. *Panorama de las ideas contemporaneas en los Estados Unidos*. *The Americas*, XVI (October, 1959), 186-91.

Cuneo, J. R. *Robert Rogers of the Rangers*. *Pennsylvania Maga-*

zine of History and Biography, LXXXIV (January, 1960), 99-100.

Sterling, R. W. *Ethics in a World of Power. The Political Ideas of Friedrich Meinecke. World Affairs Quarterly*, XXX (January, 1960), 379-81.

Wainwright, N. B. *George Croghan: Wilderness Diplomat. American Historical Review*, LXV (January, 1960), 429.

Mitchell, B. *Alexander Hamilton: Youth to Maturity, 1755-1788* (Vol. I). *Science and Society*, XXIV (Winter, 1960), 83-85.

Perry, R. L. (ed.). *Sources of Our Liberties; Documentary Origins of Individual Liberties in the United States Constitution and Bill of Rights. Pacific Northwest Quarterly*, LI (April, 1960), 91.

Eccles, W. J. *Frontenac: The Courtier Governor. Journal of Modern History*, XXXII (June, 1960), 158-59.

Labaree, L. W. *et al.* (eds.). *The Papers of Benjamin Franklin* (Vol. I). *American Historical Review*, LXVI (October, 1960), 170-71.

Boyd, J. P. (ed.). *The Articles of Confederation and Perpetual Union. New England Quarterly*, XXXIII (December, 1960), 556-57.

Hyman, H. M. *To Try Men's Souls. Pacific Northwest Quarterly*, LII (April, 1961), 76-77.

Labaree, L. W. *et al.* (eds.). *The Papers of Benjamin Franklin* (Vol. II). *American Historical Review*, LXVI (April, 1961), 750-52.

Goff, F. R. (ed.). *The Primordia of Bishop White Kennett; The First English Bibliography of America. Inter-American Review of Bibliography*, XI (April-June, 1961), 157-58.

Thomas, D. H., and L. M. Case (eds.). *Guide to the Diplomatic Archives of Western Europe. Pacific Northwest Quarterly*, LII (July, 1961), 125.

Shipton, C. K. *Sibley's Harvard Graduates* (Vol. XI, *Biographical Sketches of Those Who Attended Harvard College in the Classes 1741-1745, with Bibliographical and Other Notes*).

Bibliography

Mississippi Valley Historical Review, XLVIII (September, 1961), 299-300.

Gilbert, F. *To the Farewell Address. Annals of the American Academy of Political and Social Science*, CCCXL (March, 1962), 154-55.

Wright, E. *Fabric of Freedom, 1763-1800. Mississippi Valley Historical Review*, XLIX (June, 1962), 109-10.

Bernstein, H. *Making an Inter-American Mind. Hispanic American Historical Review*, XLII (November, 1962), 582-83.

Sosin, J. M. *Whitehall and the Wilderness: The Middle West in British Colonial Policy, 1760-1775. Indiana Magazine of History*, LVIII (December, 1962), 374-76.

Crick, B. R., and M. Alman (eds.). *A Guide to Manuscripts Relating to America in Great Britain and Ireland. Pacific Northwest Quarterly*, LIV (January, 1963), 44-45.

Labaree, L. W. *et al.* (eds.). *The Papers of Benjamin Franklin* (Vols. IV-V). *American Historical Review*, LXVIII (April, 1963), 762-65.

Shipton, C. K. *Sibley's Harvard Graduates* (Vol. XII, *Biographical Sketches of Those Who Attended Harvard College in the Classes 1746-1750, with Bibliographical and Other Notes*). *Mississippi Valley Historical Review*, L (June, 1963), 111-12.

Labaree, L. W. *et al.* (eds.). *The Papers of Benjamin Franklin* (Vol. VI). *American Historical Review*, LXIX (October, 1963), 162-63.

Borning, B. C. *The Political and Social Thought of Charles A. Beard. Western Humanities Review*, XVIII (Spring, 1964), 176-78.

Klein, M. M. (ed.). *The Independent Reflector Or Weekly Essays on Sundry Important Subjects More particularly adapted to the Province of New-York. William and Mary Quarterly*, 3rd Series, XXI (July, 1964), 457-60.

Shipton, C. K. *New England Life in the 18th Century : Representative Biographies From Sibley's Harvard Graduates. Journal of American History*, LI (September, 1964), 294-95.

Bibliography

Labaree, L. W. *et al.* (eds.). *The Papers of Benjamin Franklin* (Vol. VII). *American Historical Review,* LXX (October, 1964), 183-86.

Hall, M. C., L. H. Leder and M. S. Kammen (eds.). *The Glorious Revolution in America. North Carolina Historical Review,* XLII (January, 1965), 114-16.

MacKesy, P. *The War for America, 1775-1783. Annals of the American Academy of Political and Social Science,* CCCLVII (January, 1965), 194-95.

Labaree, L. W. *et al.* (eds.). *The Autobiography of Benjamin Franklin. American Historical Review,* LXX (April, 1965), 804-6.

Jones, H. M. *O Strange New World. New York Historical Society Quarterly,* XLIX (July, 1965), 306-8 (review written with Margaret Fisher).

Tansill, C. C. *The Secret Loves of the Founding Fathers. American Historical Review,* LXX (July, 1965), 1129-31 (review written with Margaret Fisher).

Hanna, W. S. *Benjamin Franklin and Pennsylvania Politics. American Notes and Queries,* IV (November, 1965), 44-46.